Ander Berrojalbiz

Sources from the Dawn of the Great Witch Hunt in Lower Navarre, 1370

Akelarre

palgrave
macmillan

Ander Berrojalbiz
Durango, Spain

ISSN 2731-5630　　　　　ISSN 2731-5649　(electronic)
Palgrave Historical Studies in Witchcraft and Magic
ISBN 978-3-031-15812-4　　　ISBN 978-3-031-15813-1　(eBook)
https://doi.org/10.1007/978-3-031-15813-1

Translation from the Spanish language edition: "Akelarre. Historias nocturnas en los albores de la gran caza de brujas" by Ander Berrojalbiz, © Pamiela 2021. Published by Pamiela. All Rights Reserved.
© The Author(s), under exclusive license to Springer Nature Switzerland AG 2023
This work is subject to copyright. All rights are solely and exclusively licensed by the Publisher, whether the whole or part of the material is concerned, specifically the rights of reprinting, reuse of illustrations, recitation, broadcasting, reproduction on microfilms or in any other physical way, and transmission or information storage and retrieval, electronic adaptation, computer software, or by similar or dissimilar methodology now known or hereafter developed.
The use of general descriptive names, registered names, trademarks, service marks, etc. in this publication does not imply, even in the absence of a specific statement, that such names are exempt from the relevant protective laws and regulations and therefore free for general use.
The publisher, the authors, and the editors are safe to assume that the advice and information in this book are believed to be true and accurate at the date of publication. Neither the publisher nor the authors or the editors give a warranty, expressed or implied, with respect to the material contained herein or for any errors or omissions that may have been made. The publisher remains neutral with regard to jurisdictional claims in published maps and institutional affiliations.

Cover illustration: Pictorial Press Ltd/Alamy Stock Photo

This Palgrave Macmillan imprint is published by the registered company Springer Nature Switzerland AG
The registered company address is: Gewerbestrasse 11, 6330 Cham, Switzerland

To Maider

Note for the English Edition

This book presents the only two extant documents on the sorcery trial of Pes de Guoythie and Condesse de Beheythie, held in Lower Navarre in 1370. The first version of this text was read at the 11th International Conference of the AKIH (Arbeitskreis für Interdisziplinäre Hexenforshung), devoted to *Witches and Animals. The Animal Turn in Witchcraft Studies* (25–28 September 2019, Weingarten, Germany). Then, it was developed as a book and published in Spanish, in 2021, by the Basque publishing house Pamiela, under the title *Akelarre. Historias nocturnas en los albores de la gran caza de brujas*. Now, thanks to an offer made by Willem de Blécourt and his fellow editors Jonathan Barry and Owen Davies, the book has been corrected, translated and adapted (some parts have been reorganised or rewritten), comprising colour photographic reproductions and full transcriptions of both of the 1370 sources as well as an extensive discussion and contextualisation, which includes English translations of the most salient passages of both documents and which places a special emphasis on little-known Basque and Pyrenean evidence from between the fourteenth and seventeenth centuries.

Durango
April 2022

Contents

Sources from the Dawn of the Great Witch Hunt in Lower Navarre, 1370   1
1. Sorceresses and Potion Givers   3
2. An Unknown Article   6
3. Sentence   9
4. Ordeal   10
5. Torture   12
6. Metamorphosis and Child-Killing   13
7. Poisoned Apples   18
8. Toads and Ferns   22
9. Boquelane   25
10. Lane de Boc   27
11. Boc de Biterna   34
12. May de Biterna   41
13. The Mother of God   43
14. The Deviless   44
15. Aquerlarre   46
16. An Unknown Lacuna   58

AGN, Comptos, Documentos, caj. 87, no. 62, 2   65
AGN, Comptos, Documentos, caj. 87, no. 62, 1   72

Bibliography   73

Index   79

List of Maps

Map 1   The Kingdom of Navarre in the High Middle Ages   2
Map 2   The circumscriptions of Lower Navarre in the fourteenth
        century   4

Sources from the Dawn of the Great Witch Hunt in Lower Navarre, 1370

Akelarre

Abstract This book provides an annotated source edition of the only two extant documents related to the sorcery trial brought against Pes de Guoythie and Condesse de Beheythie in Lower Navarre, in 1370. It provides full transcriptions of both documents, and English translations of the most salient passages. These sources illustrate at an early date many of the features prevalent in later documents on whitch trials, such as the metamorphosis of those accused into animals; infanticide; poisoned apples; collective meetings; and ointments made from various creatures. As such, it offers a fascinating insight into allegations of witchcraft in the High and Late Middle Ages.

Keywords Sorcery · Witchcraft · Middle Ages · Pyrenees · Metamorphosis · Akelarre

In an often-cited article, "'Many reasons why': witchcraft and the problems of multiple explanation" (1996), Robin Briggs wrote: "Certainly there is not much hope that new evidence will transform the situation in some dramatic fashion".[1]

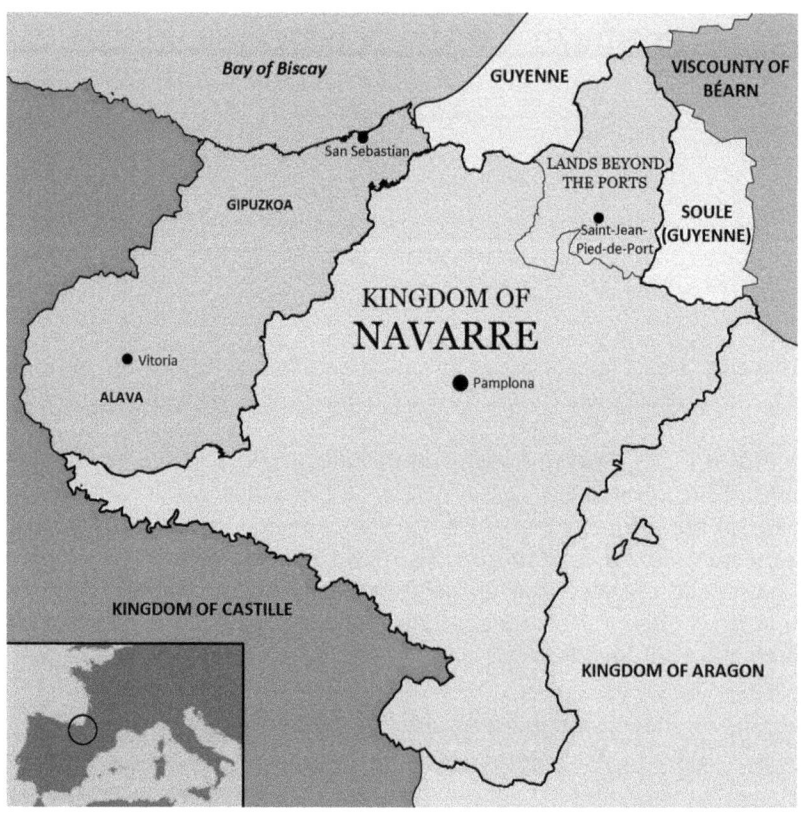

Map 1   The Kingdom of Navarre in the High Middle Ages[2]

---

[1] Robin BRIGGS, «"Many reasons why": witchcraft and the problems of multiple explanation» in Jonathan BARRY, Marianne HESTER and Gareth ROBERTS (eds.), *Witchcraft in Early Modern Europe: Studies in Culture and Belief*, Cambridge, Cambridge University Press (Past and Present Publications), 1996, p. 50.

[2] https://es.wikipedia.org/wiki/Reino_de_Navarra#/media/Archivo:Reino_de_Navarra_Sancho_VII_el_Fuerte.svg; this map has a Creative Commons license CC BY 3.0; it has been modified according to the purposes of this book.

This book presents what I think is important new evidence. Time will tell if it provokes any kind of transformation, and if so, how dramatic it will be.

1 Sorceresses and Potion Givers

Lower Navarre or *Tierras de Ultrapuertos* ('The Lands beyond the Ports'), as it used to be known in the fourteenth century, comprised the lands of the Kingdom of Navarre north of the Pyrenees (see Map 1). The Basque language was in common use in those lands while Gascon-Occitan prevailed in administrative use along with Navarrese Romance and Latin. Some of these territories were under the direct dominion of the crown (the Bailiwick of La Bastide-Clairence and the Castellany of Saint-Jean, the latter comprising the lands of Cize, Ossès and Arberoue plus the parishes of Irissarry, Iholdy and Armendarits), and others belonged to different lords who paid homage and swore fealty to the King of Navarre (Baïgorry, Lantabat, Agramont, Mixe and Ostabarret; see Map 2). For example, the lands of Mixe and Ostabarret belonged to the Viscount of Tartas, whose other dominions were outside of the kingdom.

Although they are comparatively early, the documents from 1370 that will be analysed in the following pages are not the earliest extant sources on sorcery in Lower Navarre. The Royal and General Archive of Navarre (AGN) in Pamplona preserves a series of accounting records from the thirteenth and fourteenth centuries corresponding to the territories under the direct control of the Navarrese crown. Included in these, among many other data, one can find accounts relating to the administration of justice. The information for Lower Navarre begins with rather irregular records about the Castellany of Saint-Jean between 1280 and 1329. Then, between 1329 and 1349, the records become regular on an annual or biannual basis and also include the Bailiwick of La Bastide-Clairence. Finally, due to a short-lived change of jurisdiction, records are kept for the regions of Mixe and Ostabarret for the years between 1338 and 1349.

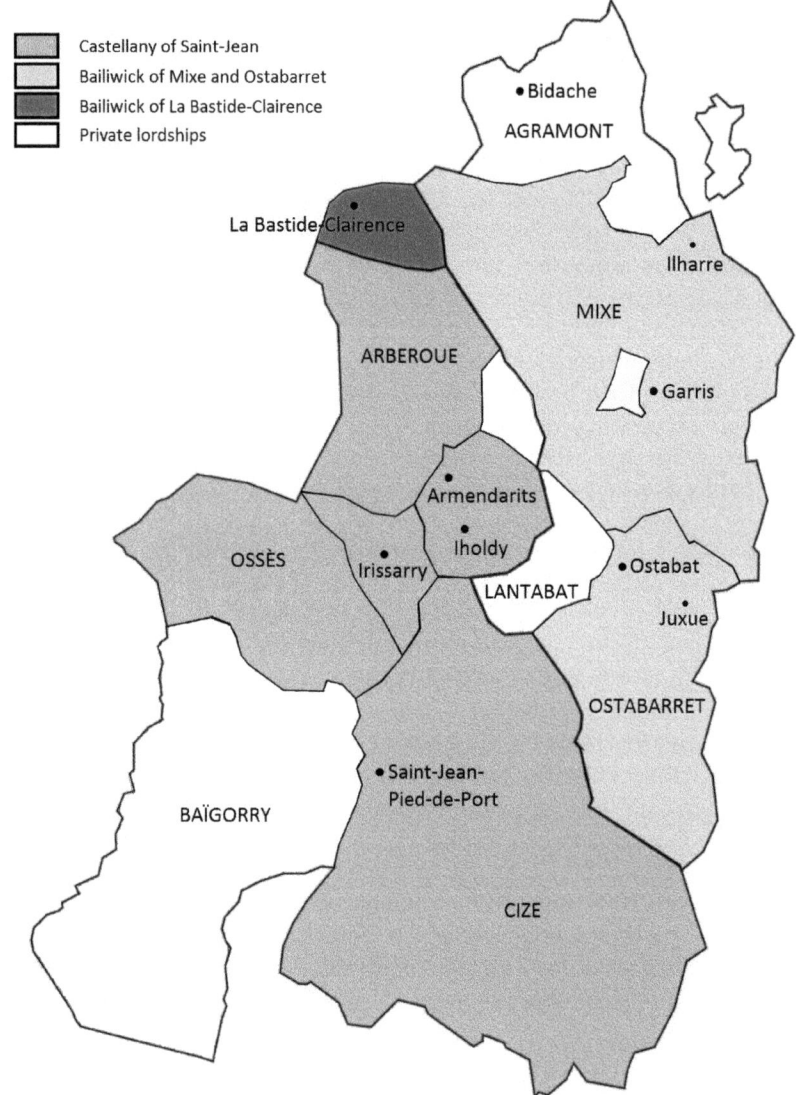

Map 2 The circumscriptions of Lower Navarre in the fourteenth century[3]

[3] https://es.wikipedia.org/wiki/Baja_Navarra#/media/Archivo:Circunscripc iones_de_Tierras_de_Ultrapuertos_(Baja_Navarra)_-_Siglo_XIV.jpg; this map has a Creative Commons license CC BY-SA 4.0; it has been modified according to the purposes of this book.

After this date, data concerning the administration of justice practically disappears for the territories north of the Pyrenees.[4]

One of these records shows that in 1314, "two women from the land of Cize were arrested and brought to justice; who were *herboleras* and who did a lot of harm and killed other women with bad herbs and bad artifices; who were in prison for 15 days, until the truth about their evil doings was known from them; these women were burnt".[5]

Further on, these concise notes indicate that between 1329 and 1342, another thirteen women were tried by the secular courts beyond the Ports under the accusations of being *"faytilheras"* and *"herboleras"* (the records in Latin translate these two concepts as *"sortilegas"* and *"datrices potionum"*, this is, 'sorceresses' and 'potion givers'). The seriousness with which the Navarrese authorities north of the Pyrenees took the alleged powers of these women is shown in the two records where we are told that more than fifteen men were sent to arrest a single woman and that a spy was paid to lure her to the place where she was to be captured. At least twelve of these women were burnt at the stake: six were executed in La Bastide-Clairence, four in the marketplace of Saint-Jean-Pied-de-Port and two more in the marketplace of Garris, in the land of Mixe.[6]

The high number of Lower Navarrese cases—comparable only with the number of trials recorded in this period in Gourdon-en-Quercy (France)[7]—is even more striking in relation to the total absence of such

---

[4] Félix SEGURA, «Hechicería y brujería en la Navarra medieval. De la superstición al castigo», *Revista internacional de los estudios vascos* (RIEV), no. 9, 2012, pp. 284–304; Florencio IDOATE, *Catálogo del Archivo General de Navarra. Sección de Comptos. Registros*, vol. LI (1258–1364) and vol. LII (1364–1535), Pamplona, Editorial Aramburu, 1974.

[5] «*Por dos mugeres de la terra de Çisa qui fueron presas et justiçiadas, las quoales eran herboleras e qui muyto de mal fizieron et mataron otras mugeres con yherbas malas et por malos engenios; las quoales estidieron en preson XV dias, ata tanto que d'eyllas fuesse sabida la verdat de los malefiçios que feyto auian; las quoales mugeres fueron quemadas. Con leynna, con cadenas et con palos comprados et con el loguerio de los hombres que les dauan el fuego et con la expensa que fizieron en la preson, XL sueldos*»; Archivo General de Navarra (AGN), Comptos, reg. 43, f. 168v.

[6] AGN, Comptos, reg. 24, ff. 76v and 78r; reg. 25, f. 244r; reg. 26, ff. 213v and 214r; reg. 36, f. 104r; reg. 39, f. 83v; reg. 40, f. 222r; reg. 46, ff. 80v and 86v; reg. 47, ff. 231r and 251r. For the records on the mentioned arrests, see AGN, Comptos, reg. 25, f. 244r and reg. 26, f. 214r.

[7] Annie CHARNAY, «Sept sorcières de Gourdon au début du XIVe siècle», *Bulletin de la Société des études du Lot*, CXV, 1994, pp. 17–49.

cases in the Navarrese lands south of the Pyrenees. The AGN also holds records of the administration of justice in Upper Navarre during the first fifty years of the fourteenth century; however, in the entire fifty-year period, one can only find a single example of sorcerous activity, where in 1300 a fine was imposed upon a Jewess of Viana who performed "sorceries and enchantments".[8]

Thus, the judicial persecution of sorcery in Lower Navarre seems not so much a whim of the documentary deposit as a historical and geographical specificity, at least in relation to Upper Navarre during the first half of the fourteenth century.

2 An Unknown Article

In 1971, the Basque-French historian Eugène Goyheneche published an article about a sorcery trial in Lower Navarre. His sources were two documents, dated to 1370, which he found in the AGN and transcribed at the end of the article. The first is a page of a letter written in Gascon-Occitan and sent by Bernat Santz de Lacxaga, Bailiff of Mixe, to Martin de Artieda, Governor of Navarre. The second contains a copy of the reply sent by the Queen Regent Joan of Valois, written in Navarrese Romance.[9]

The letter—which, as published by Goyheneche, is missing the beginning and the end—is an appeal against the verdict of a trial for sorcery held in the Court of Mixe. The accused were Pes, son of the house of Guoythie, and Condesse, mistress of the house of Beheythie, both parishioners of Ilharre (a small village on the north-eastern border of the land of Mixe, adjoining the Viscounty of Béarn; see Map 2).

In this first document, we read that a third person, Willem Arnaut, son of the house of Ilharrart, also from Ilharre, was condemned to death for the murder of his niece Peyrone, mistress of Ilharrart. Willem Arnaut was supposed to be Peyrone's guardian and administrator, and the murder was apparently "due to a love affair". Before his death by hanging, Willem

---

[8] «De quidam hebrea de Viana, infamata quod faciebat sorcerias et incantaciones, et non constabat in veritate»; Florencio IDOATE, *La brujería en Navarra y sus documentos*, Pamplona, Institución Príncipe de Viana, 1978, p. 15; Roberto CIGANDA, «Introducción» in *Archivo General de Navarra. Sección de Comptos. Registro n.º 7 (1300)*, San Sebastian, Eusko Ikaskuntza (Fuentes Documentales Medievales del País Vasco, 129), 2006, p. XI.

[9] Eugène GOYHENECHE, «Un procès de sorcellerie à Ilharre en 1370», *Munibe*, XXIII, no. 4, 1971, pp. 457–461.

Arnaut confessed that he was a sorcerer (*"faytiler"*), and that he had participated with Pes and Condesse in the murder of a child, the son of Guixon d'Eliçague and Domenge, his wife. Willem Arnaut explained that, at midnight, when they were in front of the house of Eliçague, Condesse entered "under the floor of the house in the form of a dog" and strangled the child. The transcript published by Goyheneche is interrupted few lines later.

Thanks to the reply of the Queen Regent, resident at the court in Pamplona, we know that Pes and Condesse were sentenced to ordeal by hot iron, as we shall see below, and that, before answering the appeal, the regent requested that both defendants be sent to court to clarify certain "dubious things written in the proceedings" before her and the members of her council. One of the Queen's main counsellors was Bernat Folcaut, Bishop of Pamplona, who lived his latter years (he died in 1377) in exile at the papal court in Avignon.[10]

Goyheneche's article, written in French for a journal published in San Sebastian, has not been cited once, as far as I know. In fact, not even Goyheneche himself realised the true importance of the documents, although it is true that at the time of their publication, in 1971, they did not seem as early as they do today. This was because Norman Cohn had not yet proved that several renowned Italian and French witchcraft trials—supposedly dating from the late thirteenth and mid-fourteenth centuries—were actually forgeries. Cohn presented this evidence in his book *Europe's Inner Demons*, published in 1975.[11] Once this happened, the trial of Pes and Condesse became, to the best of my knowledge, the earliest surviving court case in which accusations of animal metamorphosis and infanticide were recorded, two accusations that would play a prominent role in witchcraft trials from the fifteenth to the seventeenth centuries throughout Europe.

In a footnote at the end of his article, Goyheneche thanks Florencio Idoate, Director of the AGN, for supervising the transcription of the documents. Curiously, in his book *La brujería en Navarra y sus documentos* (1978), Idoate also deals briefly with the case of Pes and Condesse, but does not mention Goyheneche's article. What is more,

---

[10] Fernando SÁNCHEZ, *Carlos II de Navarra. El rey que pudo dominar Europa*, Pamplona, Mintzoa, 2021, p. 95.

[11] Norman COHN, *Europe's Inner Demons*, London, Pimlico, 1993, pp. 181–201.

Idoate transcribes a fragment of the letter sent by the Bailiff of Mixe that differs from the one published by Goyheneche and, in addition to commenting on the poor state of the original documents, provides details of the process that do not appear in any of the transcribed fragments.[12] Yet, inexplicably, there is no mention of Condesse's supposed metamorphosis. Moreover, it is likely that, besides the difficulty of the Gascon language and the poor condition of the documents, the apparent lack of interest in both the fragment copied by the Director of the Archive and his comments on the process has kept historians away from reading the originals until now. Be that as it may, in my case, knowing both Goyheneche's article and Cohn's work, the passages in Idoate's book meant that there was a possibility that the archive in Pamplona held more fragments of the letter, as yet unpublished and perhaps of great importance.

Indeed, under the reference number indicated by Goyheneche and Idoate, in addition to the copy of the reply sent by Joan of Valois and the page of the letter sent by the Bailiff and transcribed by Goyheneche, the Navarrese archive holds another three pages of the latter.[13]

The document is not a copy, but a fourteenth-century original dated 24 August 1370. The four pages of the letter were sewn together to form a roll which was then sealed. However, marks on its side seem to indicate that at some point, the first page was separated from the rest and sewn to the copy of the reply sent by the Queen (this may be the reason why Goyheneche only noticed these two sheets). A much-deteriorated note on the back of this first page states that the process was "seen" in the year 1376; this might be because the process had not yet been concluded or because it was used as jurisprudence in some other trial held that year. In any case, although the beginning is missing, the page transcribed by Goyheneche—certainly in a very poor state of preservation—is probably the first page of the letter, while the other three complete and end the missive. These three pages contain the confessions made by Pes and Condesse, the plea of their defender and the verdict of the court, all as part of the appeal requested by the procurator of the Lord of Mixe and communicated by the Bailiff Bernat Santz de Lacxaga to the Court of Navarre in Pamplona.

---

[12] Florencio IDOATE, *La brujería en Navarra...*, *op. cit.*, pp. 13–15 and 247–248.
[13] AGN, Comptos, Documentos, caj. 87, no. 62.

In the following sections, I will analyse what I think are the most relevant passages of this letter, paying special attention to the confessions of Willem Arnaut, Pes and Condesse. For my analysis, I have chosen to start from the end, the verdict, and work backwards through the content of the appeal. Yet, in order to facilitate future research—which may be fruitful, for example, in the analysis of the judicial process, which will only be dealt with briefly here—at the end of the book, the reader will find colour photographic reproductions and a complete transcription of both the letter of appeal and the Queen's reply. The documents have been transcribed by the palaeographer Roberto Ciganda, the main expert on medieval documents written in Gascon-Occitan working at the AGN.

3 SENTENCE

According to the letter of appeal, the Lord of Mixe, Arnaut Amanieu d'Albret, asked the Court of Mixe, located in Garris, to prosecute Pes de Guoythie and Condesse de Beheythie. The case was to be based on the confessions made by Pes and Condesse after their arrest and on the accusations of sorcery and murder pronounced by Willem Arnaut d'Ilharrart. In this regard, it should be noted that the General Charter of Navarre ('Fuero General de Navarra') stated that "the testimony of murderers was not accepted" (*"los homizieros non son recebidos en testimonianza"*), and Willem Arnaut had been condemned to death for the murder of his niece.[14]

In fact, this circumstance clearly conditioned the judgement, for which there was no consensus. Therefore:

> The minor part of the Court [of Mixe] considered it to be just that, since [Pes de Guoythie and Condesse de Beheythie] have no other accuser except the lord's procurator [because Willem Arnaut d'Ilharrart died on the gallows, condemned for murder], [and] that no accusation of the lord should harm his subjects if there were no other accuser [...], they should go free.[15]

---

[14] Pablo ILARREGUI and Segundo LAPUERTA (dirs.), *Fuero General de Navarra*, Pamplona, Imprenta Provincial, 1869, lib. II, tít. VI, cap. X, p. 29.

[15] *«La menor parthide de la cort deu per judici que puys autre acusador no han sauban lo procurador deu seynnor, que nuylhe acusation deu seynnor no deu perjudicar a son subgit si no que abos autre acusador [...] lo dam per quitis»*; AGN, Comptos, Documentos, caj. 87, no. 62, f. 4r.

However, this was not the view of the majority:

> The major part of the Court of Mixe considered it to be just that, for the confession made by Willem Arnaut, son of Ilharrart, made at his end, that the said Willem Arnaut and Pes, son of Guoythie, and Condesse, mistress of Beheythie, had put to death the son of Guixon d'Eliçague and of Domenge, his wife, and were sorcerers [*faytilers*'] and [had made use of] *faytiles* ['spells', 'bewitchments'], that the said Pes and Condesse go to Hurcoyn one month after the day of the date of this document and carry the hot iron. That there, if they are not tortured or found responsible for the aforementioned death [...], and [it is proved] that they are not sorcerers nor have ever made use of *faytiles*, but rather are good and loyal [...], that they be set free. In the case they are not proved to be good and loyal, let the lord do justice to [i.e. execute] their bodies as befits the case.[16]

The "majority" of the Court of Mixe then emphasised that this sentence was due to "the accusation of the said death by *faytiles*", implying that sorcery would justify their exceptional interpretation of the law and custom.[17]

4 Ordeal

We have just seen that the verdict of the majority of the judges condemned Pes and Condesse to undergo the hot iron ordeal. In the Kingdom of Navarre, this ordeal or "God's judgment" took place at the basilica of San Esteban in Orkoien ("Hurcoyn" in the document), five kilometres from Pamplona. The General Charter of Navarre describes a complex ritual, the core of which consisted in walking three steps carrying

---

[16] «[...] la mayor parthide de la Cort de Micxe deu per judicii tant per la confession dite per Willem Arnaut filli d'Ilharrart, feyte a sa fin, que lo dit Willem Arnaut e Pes filli de Guoythie e Condesse, daune de Beheytie, aben mort l'enfant de Guixon d'Eliçague e de Domenge, sa moylher, et heren faytiles e faytileres, que lo dit Pes e Condesse bayhen a Hurcoyn do die de la date de queste carte en vn mes et aqui leuien lo fer caut; que ay, si etz no son tortures ni merentz de la dite mort deu dit filli de Guixon de Eliçague, acusatz e confessatz per lo dit Willem Arnalt, filli d'Ilharrart, ni etz no son faytiles, ni nustemps no an vsat de faytiles far, abantz son bo[n]s e leyaus; e si parasce son per taus prauhatz bons, que sien quitis; en lo cas que no sien prauhatz per bons ni per leyaus, que lo seynnor ne faze justizie de los cos segunt au cas aparthiey»; ibidem.

[17] «E si no fos per l'acusation de la dite mort per arrazon de las faytilles [...]»; ibidem.

a red-hot iron, and the evaluation of the injuries three days later in order to interpret the divine will.[18]

Nevertheless, the use of "God's judgment" in cases of sorcery, and specifically the hot iron ordeal, was a centuries-old custom not exclusive to the Kingdom of Navarre. In a Frankish charter of 873, for example, we read that, in cases of sorcery, those who "are suspected or are under accusation [...] and it is not possible to prove their guilt with truthful witnesses, shall be subjected to the judgment of God",[19] while the Charter of Cuenca, from the end of the twelfth century, states: "The woman who is a *herbolaria* or a sorceress shall be burnt or shall save herself by hot iron".[20]

Certainly, the expression "shall save herself" is striking, but it would seem that the possibility of passing the ordeal successfully was not so remote. For instance, the historians Kerr, Forsyth and Plyley refer to three cases in late twelfth-century England in which three women—one of them tried for sorcery—overcame this ordeal[21]; furthermore, the *Regestrum Varadinense*, which records hot iron ordeals undertaken between 1208 and 1235 at the basilica of Nagyvárad, Hungary (modern-day Oradea, Romania), shows that 130 out of 208 defendants passed the test.[22] In fact, in the process against Pes and Condesse, this must have been the fear of Johan de Sormendi (procurator of the Lord of Mixe), since, not satisfied with "the judgments and sentences of the major and minor parts" of the Court of Mixe, he himself asked for the case to be revised at the

---

[18] Pablo ILARREGUI and Segundo LAPUERTA (dirs.), *Fuero General de Navarra*, op. cit., lib. V, tít. III, caps. XIII–XV, pp. 102–103.

[19] «*Si vero nominati vel suspecti, & necdum inde comprobati sunt, vel per testes veraces inde comprobari non possunt, Dei judicio examinentur*»; Etienne BALUZE, *Capitularia Regum Francorum*, II, Paris, Pierre de Chiniac, 1677, col. 231.

[20] «*DE VENEFICIIS ET FACTICIOSIS. Mulier que herbolaria vel facticiosa fuerit, comburatur, vel salvet se per [cadens] ferrum*»; José SARRIÓN, «Encantamientos, herbolarias y hechiceras en el Fuero de Cuenca y en los de su familia» in Javier ALVARADO (coord.), *Espacios y fueros en Castilla-La Mancha (siglos XI-XV). Una perspectiva metodológica*, Madrid, Ediciones Polifemo, 1995, p. 390.

[21] Margaret H. KERR, Richard D. FORSYTH and Michael J. PLYLEY, «Cold Water and Hot Iron. Trial by Ordeal in England», *The Journal of Interdisciplinary History*, XXII, no. 4, 1992, p. 579.

[22] Peter T. LEESON, «Ordeals», *The Journal of Law and Economics*, vol. 55, no. 3, August 2012, p. 706.

Court of Navarre, in Pamplona, giving rise to the writing of the document analysed here.[23]

5 TORTURE

Prior to the aforementioned verdict, the appeal brief provides us with the arguments of the defence through the mouth of the lawyer Menaut de Picassany. The plea focuses on two facts. Firstly, Picassany recalls that Willem Arnaut was hanged for the murder of his niece Peyrone, and therefore his testimony "is null and void because such is the law and custom, that no traitor should be heard and his testimony should be of no value". Moreover, he adds that "the said Willem Arnaut had ill will towards the said Pes and Condesse because they were aware of the death done [presumably he is referring again to the murder of Peyrone d'Ilharrart]".[24]

Secondly, the lawyer claims that Pes and Condesse had been tortured during the interrogations, "as evidenced by the broken limbs and badly wounded elbows", and argues that "whatever they may have said after the said abuse has no place [i.e. it is not admissible] but is null and void, both by law and by custom and for good reason". He also adds that, "as for the fact that [what they said] they said it as free people, I say it is not admissible, since, being in prison before and continuing in prison, nothing of what they said should be admissible". We can assume he means that, even if Pes and Condesse did not receive any coercion or torture at the precise moment when they made their confessions (which will be analysed in Sects. 7 to 9) before various witnesses, these should not be admitted in the trial because the defendants had just been tortured and knew that they

---

[23] *E lo dit procurador thiense per agreuiat deus judiciis e sentencies de la mayor parthide e de la meno[r] au ca e apara de la nostre cort de Micxe a la bostre bone cort de Nauarre per que suplicam a la vostre noble seynnorie que uos a cada hune de las parthides detz per sentencie co que a bos sera de bey bist de dret e d'a razon; e asignam las dites parthides que a X dies apres la date de queste carte sien per d'abant bos e porte la presente [...]*»; AGN, Comptos, Documentos, caj. 87, no. 62, f. 4r.

[24] «[...] *dic que tolu acusation feyte per lo dit Willem Arnaut aus ditz arrastatz, dic que no deu aber locg tau testimoniatge de nuyll traydor qui face tau mustration ni acusation abantz es nullc e de nullc balor, car tan es lo for e la costum, que nuylli traydor no deu esse audit ni son testimoinatge no deu baler; e si a faze, dic que es nullc e de nulle balor. E cum lo dit Willem Arnaut los portauhe malebolence au dit Pes e Condesse per co que heren sabençes de la mort feyte*»; *ibid.*, ff. 3r-4r.

would then return to prison, where they could continue to be tortured. Finally, before asking for the acquittal of Pes and Condesse, Picassany stresses that, once at the trial hearing, "when they were questioned before the full Court by the lord on each of the points they had declared, they said no and denied in the presence of the lord and the Court, because before the law and out of prison they had neither fear nor doubt".[25]

Therefore it is most likely that, hoping to put an end to the torture, both defendants confessed what they were told to confess, or what they believed their interrogators wanted to hear.

6 METAMORPHOSIS AND CHILD-KILLING

The moment has come to focus on the confessions. I shall begin with the testimony of Willem Arnaut d'Ilharrart, which led to the arrests of Pes and Condesse. His statement is dated 12 July 1370. According to the document, after stating that he was a sorcerer and that he had been initiated into the trade by Pes and Condesse, Willem Arnaut explained:

> Sir Bailiff, thus it came to pass, that in the month of May which is now past, there came to me Pes de Guoythie and Condesse, mistress of Beheythie, parishioners of Ilharre, and they told me that we should go and strangle the son of Guixon d'Eliçague and of Domenge, his wife. Those named above and the aforementioned one speaking went at midnight and, when they were at the door, the said Condesse told them to remain at the said door and that she would go in and, if she could not get out, that they should go in. After this, he said that the said Condesse was going to enter under the floor of the house in the form of a dog, and a little while later the

---

[25] «*Item a co que diitz que etz an cofessat de lor boque e an dit, dic que tau dit no a locg sauban la loi au nor car co que an diit, si dit an, an dit per force e per destrece que lo seynnor los a dat segunt dixen, lo quoau par en los menbres que son romputz e nafratz en los cos fortementz per que dic que tau dit ap[res] que abosse dit, no a locg abantz es nulle e de nulle balor etant per lo for etant per costume e per bone arazon. E a co que ditz que cum a franque persone a dit, jo dic que no car abantz estauhe en la preson et hestan en la preson, nuylli a res que dixos no deu aber locg; ne nuylle obligation que fes, ne nuylle acusation que lo procurador face ni lo seynnor, dic que no deu aber locg; e si a fey, es diz en deu esser quitis puys autre clamant ni arrancurant no an. E plus quent son enqueritz en cort pleynne per lo seynnor per cada arthicle que dit auen, dixon de no e denegan en presence deu seynnor e de la cort, car a loy heren chetz temo e chetz dopte e fore de preson*»; *ibid.*, f. 4r.

said Condesse came back down and there she said that she had strangled the said child.[26]

As we shall see in Sect. 8, Condesse confessed that these metamorphoses were carried out through the application of an ointment; she said that when they "want to take other appearances" (*"far autes semblances"*, literally, 'to make other semblances'), they "wash their hands and knees" with a "broth and, having done so, they take the appearance of dogs and cats" (*"se fen semblantz de cas e de guatz"*).

Around 1495, the Navarrese theologian Martin de Arles, partially quoting the tenth-century *Canon Episcopi*, stated that "in the Basque [*basconica*] region north of the Pyrenees", abounded women, "*maleficas* and *sortilegas*", who, deceived by the Devil, "believed that they rode at night with Diana or Herodia, that they transformed themselves into other creatures" and that they could "tear children away from their mother's milk, and then roast and eat them, or enter houses by chimneys or windows, and disturb their inhabitants in various ways".[27]

Besides, although they are not a main feature, there are several mentions of witches shapeshifting into cats or dogs in various Navarrese trials from the sixteenth and seventeenth centuries, on both sides of the

---

[26] «*Seynnor en baylle, aysi es la cause que hen lo mes de may qui passat es sim bincou a mi Pes de Guoythie e Condesse, daune de Beheythie, parropiantz d'Ilharre, e dixonme que anassem escanar l'enfant de Guixon d'Elicague e de Domenge, sa moylher, los quoaus desus nomiatz e lo predit qui parle anem la medixe noeyt e quant son en la porte bantz, dize la dite Condesse que demorassem en la dite porte e que here hentrare e, si no pode here deliurar, que etz entrassen. Apres aco, dit que ba hentrar la dite Condesse per debut lo sola de l'ostau en forme de can et hun paucg estat la dite Condesse baixir e baus dize que escanat l'abe lo dit enfant*»; ibid., f. 1r.

[27] «*Maleficas et sortilegas mulierculas, que ut plurimum vigent in regione basconica ad septentrionalem partem montium Pireneorum, que vulgariter broxe nuncupantur, [...] credentes cum Diana vel Herodia de nocturnis horis equitare vel se in alias creaturas transformare. Sed ipse sathanas, cum mentern cuiusque mulieris similis ceperit et hanc per infidelitatem sibi subiugaverit [...]. Unde quedam muliercule, inservientes sathane, demonum illusionibus seducte, credunt et profitentur nocturnis horis, cum Diana, paganorum dea, vel Venere, in magna mulierum multitudine equitare et alia nephanda agere, puta parvulos a lacte matris avellere, assare et comedere, domos per caminos seu fenestras intrare et habitantes variis modis inquietare, que omnia et consimilia solum fantastice accidunt eis*»; José GOÑI, «El tratado *De Superstitionibus* de Martín de Andosilla», *Cuadernos de etnología y etnografía de Navarra*, no. 9, 1971, pp. 276–277. For the *Canon Episcopi*, see Regino of PRÜM, «De Ecclesiasticis Disciplinis» in Jacques Paul MIGNE, *Patrologia Latina*, CXXXII, col. 352 and Jeffrey B. RUSSELL, *Witchcraft in the Middle Ages*, Ithaca-London, Cornell University Press, 1988, pp. 291–293.

Pyrenees. For example, in the documents corresponding to an enquiry carried out in 1576 in the Ultzama Valley, Upper Navarre, we read that a certain Mari Martin had gone mad after seeing her mother, Maria Gracia de Beunza, as "a vision in the form of a cat". That same year, in Ostitz, also to the south of the Pyrenees, a villager claimed to have seen some witches on a bridge in the form of "visions of dogs and cats".[28] North of the Pyrenees, the magistrate Pierre de Lancre, in his *Tableau de l'inconstance* of 1613, records that Jeannette d'Abadie, resident in Ciboure (Labourd), aged 16, declared that she had "seen witches transform themselves into wolves, dogs, cats and other animals by washing their hands with a certain water they had in a jar, and that they recovered their form when they wanted to; and so in the Sabbath, on the roads, and in every place, and being transformed they could not be seen, and nothing was seen of them but a glow".[29]

Furthermore, while cats and dogs—although these last ones are much less frequent—appear as interchangeable in Basque folk accounts about metamorphosing witches, in 1992, the ethnographer Juan Garmendia collected a remarkable narrative in Amezketa (Gipuzkoa), a village in the vicinity of the Aralar mountain range:

> A woman used to lay down facing up after having applied a sorcerous ointment on her body. Being like that, a cat figure came out of her mouth while she remained as if dead. Then, when the witch cat returned, it went back into the woman through the mouth, and she came back to life.
>
> One day, before the cat returned from the witchcraft activities, the people in the house turned over the woman's body. Seeing it like that, the cat moved back and forth until they put the body facing up again. All this happened by night.[30]

---

[28] Florencio IDOATE, *La brujería en Navarra...*, op. cit., pp. 113 and 339.

[29] «*Qu'elle a veu des sorcieres se transformer en loup, en chien, en chat & autres animaux, en se lavant les mains de quelque eau qu'elles avoient dans un pot, & reprenoyent leur forme quand bon leur sembloit: & ce au sabbat, par les chemins, & en tous lieux & estant transformees ne peuvent estre veues, & et ne voit on rien prés d'elles que quelque lueur*»; Pierre de LANCRE, *Tableau de l'inconstance des mauvais anges et demons*, Paris, Nicolas Buon, 1613, p. 134.

[30] «*Andre bat, sorginkeritzako ukendu batekin gorputza igurtzi ondoren, oheratu eta gora begira jartzen zen. Honela zegoela ahotik katu-irudi bat ateratzen zitzaion eta andrea hilda bezala geratzen zen. Katu sorgina itzultzen zenean ahotik andrearen barrura sartzen zen eta hau berriro piztu egiten zen. Behin batean, katua sorginkeriak egin ondoren kanpotik etxera bildu baino lehen, etxekoek gorputza ahuspez jarri zuten, eta honela ikusirik, katua*

Even so, the contents of these narratives about metamorphosis and child-killing can be traced a long way back through the centuries. Without trying to be exhaustive, we can start with Ovid's account about the *strix*, where a savage bird is described entering a house in order to suck the blood of a newborn child; a few lines before, Ovid wonders whether these *striges* were real birds or rather old women magically metamorphosed into birds.[31]

Apuleius, in his *Metamorphoses* or *The Golden Ass* (second century AD), also depicts women who can shape shift into animals, including dogs[32]; and some chapters later, we can read of how a woman called Pamphile metamorphosed into an owl after applying an ointment to her body.[33]

Living between the seventh and eighth centuries, John of Damascus wrote a brief treatise *On Striges*. In it, we are told:

> The ignorant say that *Striges*, who are also called *Geloudes*, are women. They allege regarding them that they appear in the air at night, and they enter houses, unimpeded by doors and their bars, they enter through secured doors, and they strangle infants. Others say that they devour their liver, and all their vital fluids, setting short limits to their lives. And they strongly maintain, by those who have seen, and others who have heard these things, that they enter houses with the doors shut, either in bodily form or with their naked soul [...] while their body is asleep on their bed.[34]

Five centuries later, Snorri Sturluson's *Ynglinga Saga* tells:

---

batera eta bestera mugitzen zen, gora begira berriro jarri arte. Gauza hauek guztiak gauez gertatutakoak dira»; Juan GARMENDIA, *Jentilak, sorginak eta beste*, San Sebastian, Elkar, 1994, pp. 30 and 91; José Miguel de BARANDIARÁN, *Brujería y brujas: Testimonios recogidos en el País Vasco*, San Sebastian, Txertoa, 1994, pp. 39–48.

[31] OVID, *Fasti*, VI, 129–168.

[32] APULEIUS, *Metamorphoseis*, II, 22.

[33] *Ibid.*, III, 21.

[34] John of DAMASCUS, «De strygibus» in Jacques Paul MIGNE, *Patrologia Graeca*, XCIV, col. 1603–1604; English translation in http://www.daimonologia.org/2018/10/on-witches-st-john-of-damascus.html [accessed 8th November 2019].

Óðinn changed shapes. Then his body lay as if it was asleep or dead, while he was a bird or an animal, a fish or a snake, and travelled in an instant to distant lands, on his own or other people's business.[35]

Also from the thirteenth century but geographically closer to our case, the following passage from Jean de Meung's *Roman de la rose* recounts:

> Many people, in their folly, think themselves *estries* by night wandering with Lady Abundance. And they say that in the whole world every third child born is of such a condition that three times a week they go just as destiny commands them; that such people push into all houses; that they fear neither keys nor bars, but enter by cracks, cat-hatches, and crevices; that their souls leave their bodies and go with the good ladies into strange places and through houses; and they prove it with such reasoning: the different things seen have not come in their beds, but through their souls, which labour and go running about thus through the world; and they make people believe that, while they are on such a journey, their souls could never re-enter their bodies if anyone had turned them over.[36]

Lastly, the French historian Annie Charnay cites a document from 1315, preserved in the archives of Gourdon-en-Quercy, according to which a woman was publicly called "old wicked child-strangler sorceress" (*"vielha malvaza fachilhiera estrangola efans"*).[37]

In addition to frightening children who did not want to sleep, it is likely that these stories served as a supernatural explanation for the

---

[35] Snorri STURLUSON, *Heimskringla*, trans. by Alison Finley and Anthony Faulkes, London, Viking Socierty for Northern Research, University College London, 2011, p. 10.

[36] «*Maintes gens, par lor folies / cuident estre par nuit estries, / erranz aveques dame Abonde; / e dient que par tout le monde / li tierz enfant de nacion / sont de cete condicion. / Qu'il vont treis feiz en la semaine / si cum destinee les maine; / e par touz ces osteus se boutent, / ne cles ne barres ne redoutent, / ainz s'en entrent par les fendaces, / par chatieres e par crevaces; / e se partent des cors les ames, / e vont avec les bonnes dames / par leus forains e par maisons; / e le pruevent par teus raisons: / car les diversitez veues / ne sont pas en lor liz venues, / ainz sont leur ames qui labeurent / e par le monde ainsinc s'en cueurent. / E tant come il sont en tel eire, / n'i ce il font aus genz acreire, / qui leur cors bestourné avrait, / jamais l'ame entrer n'i savrait*»; Ernest LANGLOIS (ed.), *Le roman de la rose*, Paris, Librairie Ancienne Édouard Champion, 1922, IV, p. 229, 18,425–18,448; English translation in Guillaume de LORRIS and Jean de MEUN, *The Romance of the Rose*, trans. by Charles Dahlberg, Princeton, Princeton University Press, 1995, pp. 305–306; the translation has been modified where necessary.

[37] Annie CHARNAY, «Sept sorcières de Gourdon...», *op. cit.*, p. 24.

sudden, incomprehensible deaths of newborn and young children, and perhaps also as alibis for the infanticide of unwanted sons or daughters.

Nevertheless, more than for the contents of the account—which probably had their origins in stories that had been told many times—Willem Arnaut's confession is important because his testimony is the earliest evidence we have of these narratives being used in a trial. In fact, as we have seen, according to the defendant Menaut de Picassany, Willem Arnaut gave his testimony motivated by his ill will towards Pes and Condesse. If this was the case, it must be noted that Willem Arnaut would expect the judges to believe his account about the metamorphosis, as they eventually did.

7 Poisoned Apples

Pes (or Pethri), son of the house of Guoythie of Ilharre, farmer, made his declaration on the 23rd July 1370, in the castle of Garris, before: Menaut, master of Naquole (Lieutenant of the Bailiff of Mixe), Bernat Santz d'Urruthie (notary public) and several witnesses. It should be remembered that, according to the defence lawyer Menaut de Picassany, these confessions were made after the defendants had been tortured in prison, and with the prospect of being imprisoned again until the trial was held. Thus, according to the document:

> The aforementioned Pes speaking said that it might well be seven or eight years ago that he met Condesse, mistress of Aguerre of Ilharrart, in a narrow street *fazen* ['doing', 'making'] *faytiles* on the sly, and the said Condesse told him that, since he had arrived there, he had better learn to cast spells [*far faytiles*] or, if he did not want to, that he would die or contract leprosy, to which Pes de Guoythie replied that he had better learn the trade.[38]

It is difficult to say what kind of spells Condesse d'Aguerre (not to be confused with the accused Condesse de Beheythie) was supposed to be casting, but the scene is somewhat reminiscent of one depicted in a trial

---

[38] «*Lo sobredit Pes qui parle dixo que bey pode abe VII o hoeyt antz que encontre Condesse daune d'Aguerre d'Ilharrart en vne carrere estrete fazen las faytiles heuba dize la dite Condesse que puys a qui here escadut bertaderementz cumbie que aprencos de far faytiles o, si no bole far, que et morire o que bador meset, lo quoau Pes de Guoythie espono que mes bole aprener domestir*»; AGN, Comptos, Documentos, caj. 87, no. 62, 2, f. 2r.

at Gourdon-en-Quercy in 1327. There, Raymonde de S. Albi, accused of sorcery, was described standing in front of the door of a house: "She was in the street, with her back uncovered, muttering and, with a stick, tracing signs and circles on the ground, with the evil intention of harming B. and his wife [the inhabitants of the house]".[39]

Besides, in Pes' story, we are struck by the presence of a particular external coercion: if Pes refuses to learn to cast spells, it will not be Condesse, the sorceress, who will kill him or give him leprosy, but such misfortunes will simply happen. This "external coercion" could be perhaps related to the "destiny" already noted in the *Roman de la rose*—under whose "command", all third sons go out three times a week with "Lady Abundance"—or to the rules or precepts governing certain beliefs—for example, the inadvisability of turning over the bodies of those whose souls "have gone out".[40]

Returning to Pes de Guoythie's confession:

> Then he said that he was there when the said Pes speaking and Willem Arnaut, son of Ilharrart, and Condesse, mistress of Beheythie of Ilharre, killed the son of Domenge d'Eliçague, from the parish of Ilharre.[41]

In this way, Pes admitted to having participated in the infanticide of which he was accused. Furthermore, he confessed to having committed two more, also implicating two other men from the region (Pejenauton [or Per Arnaut] d'Apathie and Per Arnaut de Hingoue):

> And then he acknowledged by God and by his soul the aforementioned one speaking that he and Pejenauton, master of Apathie of Ilharre, killed the child of [the house of] Ihirçe of Camou. And then he acknowledged by God and by his soul that the one speaking and Per Arnaut de Hingoue and Condesse, mistress of Beheythie of Ilharre, strangled a child in Biscay Hiriart.[42]

---

[39] Annie CHARNAY, «Sept sorcières de Gourdon...», *op. cit.*, p. 47.

[40] See n. 36 above.

[41] «*Item apres dixo que et fo au loc quent het lo dit Pes qui parle e Willem Arnaut, filli d'Ilharrart, e Condese daune de Beheytie d'Ilharre escanan l'enfant de Domenge d'Eliçague, de la parropie d'Ilharre*»; AGN, Comptos, Documentos, caj. 87, no. 62, 2, f. 2r.

[42] «*Item apres dixo a Diu e a sa anime lo predit qui parle que et e Pejenauton, seynnor d'Aphatie d'Ilharre, escanan l'enfant d'Ihirçe de Camou. Item apres dixo a Diu e a sa*

It can be imagined that the arrest of someone accused of sorcery could be used by the community, the authorities or both to hold that person responsible for the various incomprehensible deaths that had occurred in the region in recent months or years.

Subsequently, and probably in the same vein, Pes confessed to having handed out poisoned apples:

> And then he acknowledged the aforementioned one speaking that in Ilharre and in Biscay and in Sarricoete the one speaking and Willem Arnaut, son of Ilharrart, and Condesse, mistress of Beheythie, and Per Arnaut, master of Apathie of Ilharre, had handed out the poisoned apple.[43]

The exact expression in the Gascon-Occitan original is "*torude la pome d'onguan*", which literally means "to hand out the ointment apple". The expression can be misleading, but we will see how, beyond folk literature, several judicial sources from the fifteenth century relating to the eastern parts of the Pyrenees link the distribution of poisoned apples with sorcery and witchcraft.

In 1419, in Barcelona, the midwife Sança de Camins was questioned about whether "she had told someone that three women were in a company that *pomejaven* ['appled' or 'gave apples to'?] children". As in Pes de Guoythie's confession, here too it is a group or "company" which performs the action.[44]

In 1424, the legal statutes of the Vall d'Àneu (Lleida) state:

> We establish and order that if from now on we discover that any man or woman from the said valley goes with the *bruxes* [witches] by night [...], and not less if he or she *pomarà* ['apples' (as a verb) or 'gives apples to'?] or kills little children by day or night, [...] the man or woman who

---

anime que et qui parle e Perar de Huiguoe et Condesse daune de Beheytie d'Ilharre escanan vn enfant a Biscay Hiriart»; ibidem.

[43] «*Item apres dixo lo predit qui parle que Hilharre e a Biscay et a Sarricoete que et qui parle e Willem Arnalt, filli d'Ilharrart, e Condesse daune de Beheytie e Per Arnaut, seynnor d'Aphatie d'Ilharre, an torude la pome d'onguan»*; ibidem.

[44] «*Interrogada més avant si ella deposant haurie dit a neguna persona que tres dones eren de companyia que pomejaven los infants»*; Pau CASTELL, *Orígens i evolució de la cacera de bruixes a Catalunya (segles XV-XVI)*, doctoral thesis, Barcelona, Universitat de Barcelona, 2013, p. 356.

commits such crimes shall lose their body, [...] shall be burnt with fire and his or her body shall be turned to dust.⁴⁵

Lastly, we can find an enlightening case in Andorra. In the sentence of the trial for witchcraft brought against one Maria Guida in 1473, we read that the accused had "poisoned apples, of which she had given one to a certain insane person from Plandarans and another one to a child".⁴⁶

We can see that these stories about poisoned apples could serve as a complement to those about night strangulations seen in the previous section, although in this case they would not seem to serve to explain the incomprehensible or unspeakable deaths of toddlers, but those of somewhat older children, and even of some adults.

However, there may have been a grain of truth in the myth of the poisoned apple. In 1471, Margarida Soler, from Engordany, also in Andorra, accused Esclarmonda Aymar of having given her "half an apple", saying that it had "refreshed her all". The apple upset her and made her vomit. In turn, Esclarmonda confessed that Margarida "had sown discord in her house" and that, in order to punish her for it, she had "anointed" half an apple with chopped oleander and given it to her. But "as she had heard" that the oleander was very strong, "she had only anointed it a little, so as not to kill her".⁴⁷

---

⁴⁵ «*Primerament stablim e ordonam si d'aquí avant serà atrobat que hom o fembra de la dita vall vaga ab les bruxes de nit [...], e noresmeyns que pomarà o matarà inffants petits de nit o de dia, [...] que tal hom o fembra qui semblants delictes cometrà perda lo cors, [...] sia mes al foch e del seu cors feta polvera*»; Pau CASTELL, «*Sortílegas, divinatrices et fetilleres: Les origines de la sorcellerie en Catalogne*», *Cahiers de Recherches Médiévales et Humanistes*, no. 22, 2011, p. 238; English translation in Pau CASTELL, «"Wine vat witches suffocate children": The Mythical Components of the Iberian Witch», *eHumanista*, no. 26, 2014, p. 177; the translation has been modified where necessary.

⁴⁶ «[...] *insuper constet te venificasse poma ex quibus dedisse unam cuiusdam demente d'en Plandarans et alie cuidam infante*»; Pau CASTELL, *Orígens i evolució...*, op. cit., p. 425.

⁴⁷ «[...] *la dita Sclamonda donà a ella testis miga poma. [...] E la dita Sclamonda dix a ella testis: "Meya-la, que a mi tota m'a refrescada". E de ffet ella testis levors la meyà, e tentost hora per hora li solevà lo cor e vomità quant tenia al cors. [...] Et dicta Sclamonda dixit que veritat és que la dita Margarida la havie mal mesclada en casa. E axí ella deposant, per dar-li un càstich, pres miga poma e hagué un poc de baladre, e picà'l e untà'n la poma, e donà-la-li a menyar. De que ha hoyt dir és venguda en fort punt. Però que ella denunciant no la untà sinó un poc, perquè no la matàs. E més dix que vingué en fort punt, e ella testimoni deposant havie gran pahor que no murís*»; *ibid.*, pp. 365–366.

This usage of "anointing" in relation to apples could explain the expression *"pome d'onguan"* ('ointment apple') found in our document. As far as the ointment mentioned by Esclarmonda is concerned, oleander (*nerium oleander*) is a poisonous plant in all its parts, toxic even in small doses. Even the honey obtained from the nectar of its flowers seems to be able to cause serious damage to human health. The first symptoms of oleander poisoning are nausea and vomiting, followed by drowsiness, tremors, collapse and cardiac reactions such as arrhythmias, tachycardia and atrial fibrillation, which can lead to heart attacks and cardiac arrest.[48]

8 Toads and Ferns

Condesse, mistress of the house of Beheythie of Ilharre made her declaration on the same day as Pes de Guoythie, 23th July 1370:

> Condesse said that she was there with Pes de Guoythie and Willem Arnaut, son of Ilharrart, when they strangled the son of Domenge d'Eliçague of Ilharre.[49]

After admitting her involvement in the infanticide, Condesse denounced three men from the region as sorcerers (Per Arnaut d'Apathie, Per Arnaut de Hingoue and Willem Arnaut d'Etchaluçuvi),[50] and subsequently implicated them in the handing out of poisoned apples:

> And then said the aforementioned one speaking that she and Pes de Guoythie and Willem Arnaut son of Ilharrart and Per Arnaut master of Apathie, of the parish of Ilharre, and Per Arnaut master of Hingoue

---

[48] «*Nerium oleander*» in *Wikipedia*; Marc BADAL, *Cuadernos de viaje. Fragmentos y pasajes históricos sobre semillas*, San Sebastian, Haziera, 2016, pp. 162–163.

[49] «*Condesse dixo que here fo au locg am Pes de Guoythie e am Willem Arnaut filli d'Ilharrart quent escanan l'enfant de Domenge d'Eliçague d'Ilharre*»; AGN, Comptos, Documentos, caj. 87, no. 62, 2, fol. 2r.

[50] «*Item apres dixo la predite qui parle que Willem Arnaut sire d'Etchaluçuui de la parropie de Guabat es faytiler e vse de faytiles. Item dixo per medixs departhit que Per Arnaut seynnor de Hinguoe here tambey faytilere usauhe de faytiles. Item dixo per medix departhit la predite qui parle que Per Arnaut seyhnor d'Aphatie d'Ilharre here faytiler e usauhe de faytiles*»; *ibid.*, fol. 2r-3r.

and Willem Arnaut master of Etchaluçuvi of Gabat had handed out the ointment apple, that is to say, in Ilharre and in Gabat.[51]

Note that two of these names correspond to those of the two men Pes de Guoythie had already linked to two infanticides (Per Arnaut d'Apathie and Per Arnaut de Hingoue). It could be hypothesised that these names were suggested by one of the interrogators. At the very least Apathie, or Abbadie, was the surname of a wealthy and powerful family in Ilharre until the twentieth century, and the accusation of sorcery had been commonplace in political plots since the early fourteenth century.[52]

In any case, the denunciations themselves are an element to be highlighted. Although it is true that we do not know what happened to Pes and Condesse after the appeal, if they were finally condemned to the stake, these denunciations—together with the use of torture—could have cleared the way for the proliferation of similar prosecutions.

Furthermore, it is important to note that the passage about the handing out of poisoned apples presents six supposed sorcerers acting in an organised way to harm the community; in this respect, it is worth remembering that, according to a fairly widespread consensus among historians, the belief in the collective and organised practice of *maleficia* was one of the elements that contributed to the emergence of the witch archetype in the first decades of the fifteenth century.

Returning to Condesse's statement, after the denunciations and the poisoned apples, the mistress of the house of Beheythie revealed the recipe for her metamorphosis:

> And then said the aforementioned one speaking that she had taken in last Lent two toads and ferns; she boiled them and when they were cooked, she took [out] the flesh; and from that broth they made the *faytiles*; and when they want to take other appearances, they wash their hands and knees

---

[51] «*Item apres dixo la predite qui parle que here e Pethrii Guoythiie e Willem Arnaut filli d'Ilharrart e Per Arnaut seynnor d'Apathie de la parropie d'Ilharre e Per Arnaut sire de Hinguoe e Willem Arnaut sire d'Etchaluçuui de Guabat aben torude la pome d'onguan, co es assaber Hilharre e a Guabat*»; *ibid.*, fol. 3r.

[52] I am grateful to Pattu Lartigau for her information on the Abbadie family, as well as for her hospitality during my visit to Ilharre. On political plots, see Ronald HUTTON, *The Witch. A History of Fear, from Ancient Times to the Present*, New Haven-London, Yale University Press, 2018, p. 163.

with that broth and, having done so, they take the appearance of dogs and cats.[53]

The use of herbs and products collected at specific times or days of the year appears to be a recurring element in this type of recipe. In the transcription of a sermon delivered in 1427 by the Franciscan Bernardino de Siena, we read that a "*strega*" ('witch') tried in Rome "had certain jars of ointment made with herbs collected on the day of Saint John and on the day of the Assumption. [...] And they said that when they anointed themselves with it, [...] it seemed to them that they were cats".[54]

On the other hand, the *Narrative of the proceedings against Dame Alice Kyteler* (prosecuted for sorcery in Ireland in 1324) links the combined use of venomous animals like the scorpion and toxic plants such as yarrow (*achillea millefolium*) to hallucinogenic effects:

> Petronilla of Meath, an accomplice of the said Dame Alice, after being six times whipped on the order of the bishop for her sorceries, [...] admitted in front of all the clergy and people that [...] she had poured out the cocks' blood [three cocks previously sacrificed to a certain demon at a crossroads] and cut the animals into pieces, and from their intestines, with spiders and other black worms like scorpions, with a herb called milfoil as well as with other herbs and horrible worms, together with the brains and clothes of a child who had died without baptism, in the skull of a robber who had been decapitated, with the advice of the said Alice, she made many concoctions, lotions and powders, which were to cause injuries to the bodies of the faithful and arouse love and hate, and also, when particular incantations were added, to make the faces of certain women appear before certain people with horns like goats.[55]

---

[53] «*Item apres dixo la predite qui parle que here prenco per Carbeda qui passat hes, dus crepautz [e] heus, la cose e quent sen cuytz quen bagua la carn; e dequet bro fazen las faytiles; e quent se bolen far autes semblances etz, se laben dequet bro las mas e los julhs e, alox hetz, se fen semblantz de cas e de guatz*»; AGN, Comptos, Documentos, caj. 87, no. 62, 2, fol. 3r.

[54] «[...] *e ine aveva certi bossoli d'unguenti fatti d'erbe che erano colte nel dì di santo Giovanni e nel dì de la Ascensione.* [...] *E dicevano che en essi s'ugnevano, e così come erano ónte, lo'pareva èssare gatte*»; Luciano BANCHI (ed.), *Le prediche volgari di San Bernardino da Siena*, Siena, Tip. edit all'inseg. di S. Bernardino, 1888, pp. 122–123.

[55] «*Petronilla de Midia, una de sodalibus dictæ dominæ Aliciæ, quae postquam fuit sex vicibus per episcopum pro suis sortilegiis fustigata,* [...] *coram toto clero et populo fatebatur* [...] *tres optulit gallos in quadruviis extra civitatem cuidam daemoni* [...], *sanguinem*

Returning to Condesse's simpler recipe, toads and their poisonous and psychoactive properties are not a novelty in the sources about these preparations, but ferns are. In this sense, it might be worth mentioning that the lady fern (*athyrium filix-femina*)—which thiaminase content may affect human health—is known in the Basque language as *"sorgin-iratze"* ('witch-fern').[56]

9 BOQUELANE

Nevertheless, possibly the most shocking part of Condesse's statement was yet to come:

> And then she said that she had been to *boque lane* fully three times [*bey tres betz*]. And then she acknowledged by God and by her soul that she had never confessed that sin to us because she had no power to confess it. And she said that they used to go to *boquelane* on Sundays. And then she said that she did not know anything else, since she had said all she knew.[57]

---

effundendo et dividendo membratim, de quorum intestinis, cum araneis et aliis vermibus nigris ad modum scorpionum, cum quadam herba quae dicitur millefolium, et aliis herbis et vermibus detestabilibus, una cum cerebro et pannis pueri decedentis sine baptismo, in testa capitis cujusdam latronis decollati, ad informationem dictæ Aliciæ, multas fecit confectiones, pixides, et pulveres, ad affligendum corpora fidelium et amores et odia concitandum, et ut facies quarundam mulierum cum quibusdam incantationibus adjectis appareret cornutæ apud certas personas velut capræ»; Thomas WRIGHT (ed.), *A Contemporary Narrative of the Proceedings Against Dame Alice Kyteler, Prosecuted for Sorcery in 1324, by Richard de Ledrede, Bishop of Ossory*, London, The Camden Society, 1843, pp. 31–32; English translation in L. S. DAVIDSON and J. O. WARD (eds.), *The Sorcery Trial of Alice Kyteler*, Asheville, Pegasus Press, 2004, pp. 62–63; the translation has been modified where necessary.

[56] For two medieval sources on toads and how to extract their venom (containing bufotenine), see Dan ATTRELL and David PORRECA (eds.), *Picatrix. A Medieval Treatise on Astral Magic*, Pennsylvania, The Pennsylvania State University Press, 2019, p. 210. On the psychoactive effects of bufotenine (5-HO-DMT) combined with harmine or harmaline (found in various plants), see Jonathan OTT, «Pharmañopo-Psychonautics: Human Intranasal, Sublingual, Intrarectal, Pulmonary and Oral Pharmacology of Bufotenine», *Journal of Psychoactive Drugs*, vol. 33, no. 3, July–September 2001 pp. 273–281.

[57] «*Item apres dixo que here heree estade a boque lane bey tres betz. Item apres dixo a Diu e a sa anime que nustemps aquet pecat nos confesse car no abe poder de confessa. Item dize que solen anar a boquelane lo dimenx. Item apres dixo que no sabe plus car sin sabes ca bey dixo et cum deus nomiatz desus*»; AGN, Comptos, Documentos, caj. 87, no. 62, 2, fol. 3r.

But what does "*boquelane*" mean? The document includes the term twice: the first time it appears as two separate words ("*boque lane*"), while in the second one it is abbreviated and both words are joined together ("*boq̄lane*").[58] Although the document features the word "*boque*" several times in the sense of 'mouth'—always referring to the mouths of the declarants in constructions such as "he said through his mouth" or similar—given the sorcerous context (which will be further discussed in the following sections), one is inclined to think that "*boquelane*" would instead be a compound term formed by "*boq(ue)*", meaning 'buck goat' or 'he-goat' (which has equivalents in most European languages, from the Portuguese "*bode*" or the Aragonese "*boque*" to the German "*Bock*"), and "*lane*", meaning 'field', 'heath' or 'meadow'. Thus, "*boquelane*" could be translated as 'buck goat meadow' or a similar expression.

The curious thing is that, according to Gascon grammar—reinforced by various sources from the fourteenth to the seventeenth centuries—the correct form would have the reverse construction: "*lane de boc*" or "*lane de bouc*". For example, the fourteenth-century French chronicler Jean Froissart mentions at least twice a place called "Lane de Bouc" in the vicinity of Lannemezan (Gascony)[59]; and Pierre de Marca, in his *Histoire de Bearn* published in 1640, mentions a pact signed at the same "Lande de Boc" in August 1232.[60]

Most probably, the explanation for this inversion of the word order between "*boquelane*" and "*lane de boc*" is to be found in the Basque language. In Basque, we find place names with constructions such as "*Aker çaltua*", "*Aquerlurra*" and "*Aquer larre*" ("k" and "qu" are different spellings of the same phoneme and the final "a" is the singular definite article). The first toponym is documented in the Aralar mountain range as early as the eleventh century, and the other two are found in sixteenth-century sources. In all cases, the form is the same as in "*boquelane*": "*aker*"—meaning 'buck goat'—in the first place,

---

[58] In the document, the line above the "q" indicates that the word has been abbreviated.

[59] Peter AINSWORTH and Godfried CROENEN (eds.), *The Online Froissart*, version 1.5, Sheffield, HRIOnline, 2013, http://www.hrionline.ac.uk/onlinefroissart.

[60] Pierre de MARCA, *Histoire de Bearn*, Paris, Veuve Jean Camusat, 1640, p. 826.

and *"lur"*, *"larre"* or *"çaltu"*—meaning 'land', 'meadow' and 'thicket' respectively—afterwards.[61]
We might therefore be dealing with a localism of the border region between Mixe and the Béarn. Another possibility would be that, as happens in other processes (see Sect. 15 below), the confessions collected in our document from 1370 were translations into Gascon of declarations pronounced in Basque; in this case, the term *"boquelane"*—which does not appear in any other known source—could be a calque of *"Aquerlarre"*, or some other similar wording, carried out for the occasion by the notary Bernat Santz d'Urruthie.
In any case, it does not seem far-fetched to suppose that the document we are dealing with here records Condesse de Beheythie—accused of sorcery in 1370—confessing to having gone three times to a place called "Buck Goat Meadow". In fact, the sources that will be analysed in the second half of this discussion point to this spot—under the name of *"Lane de Boc"*—as the place where the witches of Lower Navarre and the surrounding area held their meetings in the fifteenth and sixteenth centuries.

10 LANE DE BOC

Unfortunately, after the aforementioned documents from the fourteenth century (accounting records and trial proceedings from 1370), there is only one extant source about sorcery or witchcraft in Lower Navarre in the fifteenth century, followed by a few reports from the sixteenth and seventeenth centuries. These latter references—collected in the works of Landemont and Bordes quoted below—are of little interest for our purposes; not so the evidence concerning the fifteenth century.

---

[61] «*In partibus Iberiae, iuxta aqua currentis, soto uno, que dicitur a rrusticis* Aker Çaltua, *nos possumus dicere saltus ircorum*»; José María LACARRA, «Privilegio de Sancho el de Peñalén, confirmando al Santuario de San Miguel in Excelsis en la posesión de todos sus bienes. Lleva la confirmación de Sancho Ramírez. Año 1074», *Boletín de la comisión de monumentos históricos y artísticos de Navarra*, no. 1, 1927, p. 560. "*Aquerlurra*" is documented in 1510 as "*Aguer lurra*", in 1556 as "*Aquerrlurra*" and in 1718 as "*Aquelurra*"; Juainas PAUL, «El aquelarre, una invención afortunada», *Gerónimo de Uztariz*, no. 23–24, 2008, p. 11; for «*Aquer larre*», see Sect. 15 below.

The source in question is an article published in 1883 by Pierre de Larremendy, curate of Garris, under the pseudonym "L'abbé Landemont". It contains a summary in French of a document in Gascon-Occitan relating to the trial of Johannette, mistress of the house of Sala of Juxue (a village in Ostabarret).[62]

The original document was part of the personal archive of Arnaud Oihenart, a seventeenth-century Souletin jurist, historian and poet. Married to Jeanne d'Orsoa, daughter of a prestigious Lower Navarrese family, Oihenart moved to Saint-Palais, in Mixe, where he lived until his death in 1663. His archive passed on to his descendants until it was inherited by Clara, eldest daughter of Léon de Lafaurie and widow of Colonel Ernesto de Brancion. This lady, ennobled with the title of Countess by Napoleon III, retired in her old age to her house in Saint-Palais. Once there, she authorised Pierre de Larremendy to examine her archives, which led to the publication of numerous valuable documents and articles such as the one under consideration here. Apparently, after the death of Mme de Brancion on the 26th June 1893, her niece Jeanne de Mendiry gave Oihenart's manuscripts—we do not know whether all or only part of them—to Paul Labrouche, also a nephew of the Countess.[63] In 1994, the philologist Ricardo Cierbide stated that, with the exception of a few documents in the hands of the Barbaste family, also Oihenart's descendants, the latter's legacy was "dispersed and impossible to study".[64]

Therefore, for the time being, Landemont's summary is the only source available for the study of Johannette de Sala's case. For this reason, it must be taken into account that we do not know which details were left out in the process of translation and synthesis and that the text has been filtered by the curate of Garris. Thus, in his writing, we read that on the 7th October 1450, "Tristan, master of Camou and Bailiff of Mixe", chaired the Court before the castle of Garris, and there it was shown that:

---

[62] L'abbé LANDEMONT (Pierre Larremendy), «Procès de sorcellerie en Basse-Navarre», *Revue de Béarn, Navarre et Lannes: partie historique de la Revue des Basses-Pyrénées et des Landes*, no. 1, 1883, pp. 49–54.

[63] Ricardo CIERBIDE, «Introducción» in Arnaud d'OIHENART, *Notitia utriusque vasconiae*, Vitoria, Parlamento Vasco, 1992, pp. 17 and 29.

[64] Ricardo CIERBIDE, «Fuentes histórico-documentales de la *Notitia utriusque vasconiae* y papeles inéditos de Arnaud d'Oihenart» in *Oihenarten laugarren mendeurrena. Cuarto centenario de Oihenart. Quatrième centenaire d'Oihénart*, Bilbao, Euskaltzaindia, 1994, p. 580.

Arnaud-Peloton, master of Sarhie [of Juxue], Bailiff of Ostabarret, had taken prisoner Johannette, mistress of the house of Sala of Juxue, accused of sorcery by the deputies of the said land. Those deputies, sixteen in number, had been in charge of making enquiries and gathering information about those who made use of bad art and *fartilherie* [sorcery].[65]

From this last sentence, it can be deduced that by 1450, at least in cases of sorcery and witchcraft, the Court of Mixe had switched to the inquisitorial rather than the accusatorial process, i.e. it was no longer necessary for a person to denounce and accuse another—thereby bearing the burden of proof—in order for the latter to be prosecuted, but rather the authorities could proactively order the investigation of crimes, accuse the alleged wrongdoers and try them.
Landemont goes on with the details of the process:

Having read the enquiry about Johannette to the said bailiff, he, on the advice of the judges of the land of Mixe, subjected the accused to questioning [the document does not record whether this interrogation was carried out by means of torture, although this was common in inquisitorial processes]; after which, she made the following confessions before the bailiff, notaries and other people:
First of all, she had been initiated into her abominable trade by Condeix, mistress of Eyherabide of Juxue; it may well be fifteen years ago. It happened near a stream called Salatipia. Condeix touched her face and hands; and by this gesture she took possession, as it were, of the spirit and will of her initiate.[66]

---

[65] «*En l'année de l'Incarnation 1450, et le 7ᵉ jour d'octobre, honorable Tristan, seigneur de Camou et bailli de la terre de Mixe, tint cour devant le château de Garris, assisté de chevaliers, d'écuyers, de bourgeois, de laboureurs, et autres bonnes gens.*
Et là-même, de la part dudit bailli, il fut exposé que: En Arnaud-Peloton, seigneur de Sarhie [maison noble, située dans la paroisse de Juxue, elle a été longtemps possédée par les seigneurs de Domezain (note by Landemont)], *bailli de la terre d'Ostabaret, lui avait amené prisonnière, Johannette, dame de la maison de Sala de Juxue, accusée de sorcellerie par les députés de ladite terre. Ces députés étaient au nombre de seize, et avaient charge de faire des recherches et prendre des informations sur ceux qui usaient de mau art et de fartilherie*»; L'abbé LANDEMONT, «Procès de sorcellerie...», *op. cit*., pp. 49–50.

[66] «*Leur enquête sur Johannette de Sala ayant été lue audit bailli, celui-ci, par le conseil des Juges de la terre de Mixe, soumit la prévenue à la question; après quoi, elle fit les aveux suivants, en présence du bailli, des notaires et autres gens:*
Et d'abord, elle avait été initiée à son abominable métier par Condeix, dame d'Eyhérabide de Juxue, il pouvait bien y avoir quinze ans de cela. C'était près du ruisseau appelé

Here we find a new initiatory scene, somewhat analogous to the one recounted by Pes de Guoythie. This time, however, there is no external coercion, but it is the mistress who bends and "takes possession" of the initiate's will.

> Three months later, on a Wednesday, the same Condeix came at night to Johannette's house, told her to follow her, and gave Johannette a powder with which they rubbed each other's feet; after which, climbing along the crane [of the fireplace], they went to a place called *Lande du Bouc*; and, yet, returned home before daylight.
> On another occasion, Johannette met the mistress of Saint-Miqueu at the Sabbath, who told her: "You lack the necessary, but I will provide it for you". And they went three times to the Sabbath together, where the *bouc* gave her three *jacques* [coins minted in the Kingdom of Aragon] as salary.
> Here the document relates, with all the seriousness that befits the minutes of a session where a death sentence is pronounced, that "the said *boc*, they kiss under the tail".[67]

After describing the witches' meetings, Landemont informs us of three evil actions confessed by the defendant: causing the contraction of a girl's leg by touching it with "a certain powder", producing the lameness of one of her own children by means of a similar "touch"—the child would die shortly afterwards—and the murder of her husband's stepmother also using "poisoned powder". We then read that Johannette declared that "the mistress of Barheix; the mistress of Negueloa; Marie, mistress of Iribarnaitzin of Bunus; the mistress of Iriart of Juxue, and others" were "*sorcières*" (it is likely that the original document said

---

Salatipia. Condeix la toucha au visage et aux mains; et, au moyen de cette passe, elle prit, pour ainsi dire, possession de l'esprit et de la volonté de son initiée»; ibid., p. 50.

[67] «*Trois mois après, un mercredi, la même Condeix vint nuitamment chez Johannette, lui dit de la suivre, et lui donna une poudre dont elles se frottèrent les pieds l'une et l'autre; après quoi, grimpant le long de la crémaillère, elles se rendirent en un endroit appelé Lande du Bouc; et, cependant, rentrèrent chez elles avant le jour.*
Une autre fois, Johannette rencontra au Sabbat la dame de Saint-Miqueu, qui lui dit: "Tu manques du nécessaire, mais je te le procurerai". Et elles allèrent trois fois au sabbat ensemble, où le bouc lui donna trois jacques pour salaire.
Ici le document relate, avec tout le sérieux qui convient au procès-verbal d'une séance où une peine capitale est prononcée, que "audit boc, lo baisan debat la code"»; *ibidem.*

"*faytilheras*"). Finally, the text indicates that the court "unanimously" condemned Johannette to death by burning at the stake.[68]

Returning now to the details about the gatherings, it is unfortunate that the text gives no further information about the nature of the *boc* or its "*Lande*". The actual presence of a *boc* recalls the enigmatic painting, probably dating from the late fourteenth century, preserved on a wooden ceiling in the church of Nossa Senhora da Oliveira in Guimarães (Portugal), which depicts three women worshipping a black buck goat standing on its hind legs, and next to them a fox hanging a rat on a gallows.[69] On the other hand, Johannette's account features at least two elements (the payment of money and the kiss "under the tail") that had been part of accusations of heresy for centuries.

As early as the eleventh century, Adémar de Chabannes wrote about certain "Manicheans" in Orleans saying that the Devil appeared to them, first in the form of an "Ethiopian" and then "in the form of an angel of light", and that "every day he gave them money".[70] In the twelfth century, Walter Map tells us of a "synagogue" or meeting of "*publicani*"—supposed Manichaean heretics—where a "black cat" would

---

[68] «*Autre méfait que Johannette confesse. Il y a près de trois ans qu'elle alla, un jour, à Iribarnégaray de Juxue. La dame de ladite maison était devant la porte, ayant une toute petite fille sur le bras, Johannette toucha la jambe de l'enfant avec une certaine poudre, et instantanément la jambe fut malade et se contracta, si bien qu'elle est encore en ce moment, plus courte que l'autre.*

Johannette par un semblable attouchement, rendit boiteux un de ses propres enfants, qui mourut bientôt après.

Elle employa aussi une poudre empoisonnée pour faire mourir la marâtre de son mari.

Enfin, elle déclare que la dame de Barheix, la dame de Néguéloa, Marie, dame d'Iribarnaitzin de Bunus, la dame d'Iriart de Juxue, et d'autres encore, qu'elle nomme, sont sorcières.

La sentence fut rigoureuse: toute la cour, unanimement, jugea et déclara que la justice du roi devait faire mourir Johannette en feu ardent, afin que Dieu fût satisfait, qu'il y eut édification pour les bons, et correction pour le méchants "qui usen de mau art, de poson et de fartilherie", *et pour que justice fût maintenue*»; *ibid.*, pp. 50–51.

[69] Luis Manuel TEIXEIRA, «As pinturas dos tectos da igreja da Colegiada de Guimarães e a sua situação no contexto da pintura medieval peninsular» in *Congresso Histórico de Guimarães e a sua Colegiada. Actas. Volume IV. Comunicações*, Guimarães, 1981, p. 465.

[70] «*Manichei* [...] *adorabant diabolum, qui primo eis in Aetyopis, deinde angeli lucis figuratione apparebat, et eis multum cotidie argentum deferebat*»; Adémar de CHABANNES, «Historia Francorum» (lib. III, cap. 59) in *Monumenta Germaniae Historica. Scriptores in folio* (MGH SS), vol. IV, Hannover, 1841, p. 143.

appear, which those attending the gathering recognised as their lord and many kissed "under the tail".[71]

This last accusation was to be a particular predilection among those who wrote against Cathars and Waldensians in the thirteenth and fourteenth centuries. For example, an extensive list of "Waldensian errors" preserved in fourteenth-century handwriting presents it alongside the practice of sexual orgies—another common accusation—and a curious feature borrowed from popular culture and destined to have great success in the literature and judicial processes of the centuries to come:

> Item, [Waldensians] have among them abominable mixture, and perverse dogmas fit for this purpose, but it is a long time since this abuse has been found in these regions.
> Item, in some other regions, a demon appears to them under the appearance and figure of a cat, which they individually kiss under the tail.
> Item, elsewhere they ride on a baton smeared with a certain ointment, and in a moment they fly to the assigned places where they want to meet. However, this cannot be found in these parts.[72]

Later, in the 1430s, the kiss on the backside would figure in several witchcraft trials along with the other features mentioned above. Thus, a 1439 supplication on a case tried in Lausanne tells of a witches' meeting presided over by "a devil in the form of an Ethiopian man seated on a high throne covered with gold and silver leaf"; this devil was kissed "in his hind

---

[71] «[...] dicti sunt Publicani vel Paterini [...], expectantes in singulis sinagogis suis singulae sedeant in silentio familiae, descenditque per funem appensum in medio mirae magnitudinis murelegus niger, [...] dominum suum [...], inventumque deosculantur quisque secundum quod ampliore fervet insania humilius, quidam pedes, plurimi sub cauda, plerique pudenda»; Walter MAP, De nugis curialium, London, Camdem Society, 1850, distinctio I, cap. XXX, pp. 61–62.

[72] «Item, habent etiam inter se mixtum abhominabile, et perversa docmata ad hoc apta, sed non reperitur quod abutantur in partibus istis a multis temporibus.
Item, in aliquibus aliis partibus apparet eis daemon sub specie et figura cati, quem sub cauda sigillatim osculantur.
Item, in aliis partibus super unum baculum certo unguento perunctum equitant, et ad loca assignata ubi voluerint congregantur inmomento dum volunt. Sed ista in istis partibus non inveniuntur»; Thomas WRIGHT and James O. HALLIWELL (eds.), Reliquiae antiquae, London, John Rusell Smith, 1845, pp. 246–248. The manuscript, of possible French origin, is part of the Cotton collection; the catalogue of the British Library, where it is kept, dates its writing to the mid-fourteenth century.

nature" by the attendants "of both sexes".[73] Besides, in the proceedings against Aymonet Maugetaz, also held in Lausanne in 1438, we read:

> And then came a black man who was the devil, and he told Aymonet that he should deny God and take him for his god, which he did. [...] Then he transformed himself into a black cat, and all those who were there came to kiss his arse; Aymonet did the same as the others. And the devil gave him five sous. [...] After this adoration, everyone, both men and women, began to mingle and copulate with each other in the manner of dogs.[74]

Shortly afterwards, around 1440, we find the "nefarious kiss" mentioned for the first time in relation to both a cat and a buck goat. The quotation is from the poem *Le champion des dames* by Martin le Franc:

> Certain nights, ten thousand hags ride on a baton from the Valpute [ancient name for the Vallouise Valley in the Hautes-Alpes] to the wicked synagogue. There, they see the devil in the form of a cat or a *bouch*, whom they kiss in the arse as a sign of obedience.[75]

Yet, all this does not necessarily mean that the *boc* is a foreign element in Lower Navarre; buck goats appear to have long been associated with divinity in the Pyrenees (even with witchcraft before Le Franc evoked it, as

---

[73] «[...] ad certum pontem ubi erat magna caterva hominum utriusque sexus discumbentium comedentium et bibentium et quidam dyabolus in specie hominis ethiopis sedens in solio alta pannis aureis et argenteis celato [...] in posteriora nature parte osculatus fuit»; Filippo TAMBURINI, «Suppliche per casi di stregoneria diabolica nei registri della Penitenzieria e conflitti inquisitoriali», *Critica storica*, no. 23, 1986, p. 622.

[74] «Et ibi venit quidam homo niger qui erat dyabolus et ipsi Aymoneto dixit quod oportebat quod ipse negaret Deum et quod caperet ipsum in deum suum; quod et fecit. [...] et postea se convertit in speciem cati negri, et omnes qui ibi erant, venerunt ad osculandum eidem in culo; et ipse eciam fecit sicut ceteri. Et dyabolus ei dedit quinque solidos. [...] et facta dicta adoratione omnes dicte gentes tam mares quam mulieres inceperunt commisceri adinvincem et cohabitare unus cum alio sicut canes»; Martine OSTORERO, Agostino PARAVICINI and Kathrin UTZ TREMP (eds.), *L'imaginaire du sabbat. Edition critique des textes les plus anciens (1430 c.–1440 c.)*, Lausanne, Cahiers lausannois d'histoire médiévale, 1999, pp. 344–347; see also *ibid.*, pp. 278–281 and 290–291.

[75] «Certaines nuis, de la Valpute / sur ung bastonnet s'en aloit / veoir la synagogue pute. / Dis mille vielles en ung fouch / y avoit il communement, / en fourme de chat ou de bouch / veans le dyable proprement / auquel baisoyent franchement / le cul en signe d'obeissance»; *ibid.*, p. 456, 17,462–17,470.

we shall see in the next section). As a curious and early example, archaeologist Julien Sacaze recorded the following Roman-Aquitanian inscription from the Larboust Valley:

> AHERBELSTE DEO SENIUS & HANNA PROCUL[I FIL(II)]... ('To the god *Aherbelste*, Senius and Hanna, Procul[us' sons]...')[76]

The Aquitanian language has been indisputably linked with Basque, and as said before, in the latter we find that "*aker*"—or "*akher*" (aspirated) north of the Pyrenees —means 'buck goat', while "*beltz*" means 'black'. This leads to the conclusion that "*Aherbelste*" could mean 'Black Buck Goat'.[77]

11 Boc de Biterna

In the early thirteenth century, the troubadours Guilhem Rainol d'At and Guilhem Magret engaged in a *tenso* or lyrical debate. In it, the latter told the former:

> You've left your monk's habit far behind, and on your pate, Guillem, you have lots of patches where masses of tufts have fallen out, you Biterna buck goat-face! [*cara de boc de Biterna!*].[78]

This "*Boc de Biterna*" does not appear again in written sources until the fifteenth century, and then it is invariably linked to witchcraft. It is found in legal codes, judicial processes, demonology treatises and poems, always in the area of influence of the central and eastern Pyrenees.

None of the references clarify the meaning of "Biterna". Historians have generally interpreted it as a toponym of uncertain location relying

---

[76] Julien SACAZE, *Inscriptions antiques des Pyrénées*, Toulouse, Imprimerie et Librairie Édouard Privat, 1892, no. 348, p. 431.

[77] EUSKALTZAINDIA (Royal Academy of the Basque Language), «aker» and «beltz», *Orotariko Euskal Hiztegia* (General Basque Dictionary), www.euskaltzaindia.eus.

[78] «*Per nos laissetz vostre floc, / et avetz el suc maynt loc, / Guillem, don ameyns maynt floc, cara de boc de Biterna!*»; Martín de RIQUER, *Los trovadores: Historia literaria y textos*, Barcelona, Ariel, 2011, p. 1245, 41–44; English translation in Ruth HARVEY and Linda PATERSON, *The Troubadour Tensos and Partimens: A Critical Edition*, Cambridge, D. S. Brewer, 2010, p. 625; the translation has been modified where necessary.

on sources in which it does not appear next to the *boc*: "An Almoravid, who also has [the lordship of] Biterna and Pamplona" we read, for example, in a thirteenth-century French *chanson de geste*.[79] Besides, the poet and lexicographer Simin Palay recorded the variant "Bitèrno" in his Gascon-French dictionary and suggested a possible connection with the term "batèrno", which he translated as '*bouleversement*' ('disruption') or '*grabuge*' ('ruckus').[80]

These translations, together with the common root '*bat*', could link this concept to the Occitan "*esbat*" (translated into French by Palay and Mistral as '*tumulte*', '*amusement*', '*folâtrerie*' or '*jeu*' ['game'] and recorded in a trial for witchcraft from 1567)[81]; to the Old French "*sabateis*" (kept in a thirteenth-century source with the sense of 'tumult' or 'big noise')[82]; to the Breton "*sabbat*", "*savar*" or "*safar*" (translated by Breton-French dictionaries as '*grand bruit* [big noise] *qui se fait avec désordre*', '*tumulte*' or '*charivari*')[83]; and to the feasting and frolicking "*sabbativis noctibus*" ('sabbatical nights') censured in a pastoral visit to Saint-Malo (Brittany) in 1434.[84]

In relation to these latter pieces of evidence, it should be noted that, before being assimilated with the aforementioned "synagogue" and taking on anti-Semitic overtones, the earliest known sources for the use of the term "*sabbat*" as "witches' meeting" are found in north-western France between 1440 and 1460.[85] Besides, it could be added that the

---

[79] «[...] *un Amoravi / qui tint Biterne et Panpelune ausi*»; Pau CASTELL, *Orígens i evolució...*, op. cit., p. 78; see *ibid.*, pp. 77–80, for various hypotheses.

[80] Simin PALAY, *Dictionnaire du béarnais et du gascon modernes*, Pau, Imprimerie Marrimpouey Jeune, 1932, vol. II, pp. 649 and 650.

[81] *Ibid.*, vol. I, p. 476; Frédéric MISTRAL, *Lou Tresor dóu Felibrige*, Aix-en-Provence, Remondet-Aubin, 1886, p. 969; see also Sect. 14, note 115, below.

[82] Pierre-François FOURNIER, «Etymologie de sabbat, "réunion rituelle de sorciers"», *Bibliothèque de l'École des chartes*, CXXXIX, no. 2, 1981, pp. 247–249.

[83] Jean François LE GONIDEC, *Dictionnaire Français-Breton*, Saint-Brieuc, L. Prud'homme, 1847, p. 722; Pierre de CHÂLONS, *Dictionnaire Breton-François du diocèse de Vannes*, Vannes, Jacques de Heuqueville, 1723, p. 147.

[84] Amaury CHAOU, «La religion souterraine à Saint-Malo en 1434», *Annales de Bretagne et des pays de l'Ouest*, CII, no. 2, 1995, pp. 107–112.

[85] Franck MERCIER and Martine OSTORERO, *L'énigme de la Vauderie de Lyon. Enquête sur l'essor de la chasse aux sorcières entre France et Empire (1430–1480)*, Florence, Sismel-Edizioni del Galluzzo (Micrologus' Library), 2015, pp. 112–115.

earliest pictorial representation of a *"charivari"* (ca. 1316) shows various participants wearing animal masks.[86]

Be that as it may, the interest of the sources about the *Boc de Biterna* goes beyond the exact meaning of this latter term. Thus, in the legal statutes of the Vall d'Àneu (year 1424), the crime of "going with the witches [*bruxes*] by night" and "taking" the *Boc de Biterna* "as lord, paying him homage and disowning the name of God" is already codified alongside poisoning and infanticide.[87]

These legal statutes justify their measures by mentioning that those crimes had been discovered in trials that had already taken place. It may be to these that the poet Jaume Roig referred when he wrote around 1459:

> With a certain melted fat, / as people say, / they make an ointment / and become *bruxes*. / They rush in the night, / many of them gather, / they abjure God, / adore a *boch*, / they all honor / his cavern / called *Biterna*. / They eat and drink, / then they take off / flying through the air, / they enter wherever they want to / without opening doors. / Many of them have been killed, / burned in the fire, / sentenced / by good trials / for those excesses, / in Catalonia.[88]

---

[86] Alexander PLUSKOWSKI, «Before the Werewolf Trials. Contextualising Shape-Changers and Animal Identities in Medieval North-Western Europe» in Willem de BLÉCOURT (ed.), *Werewolf Histories*, London-New York, Palgrave Macmillan (Palgrave Historical Studies in Witchcraft and Magic), 2015, pp. 98–102.

[87] Pau CASTELL, «*Sortílegas, divinatrices...*», *op. cit.*, p. 238; for the transcription of the passage, see note 156 below.

[88] «*Ab çert greix fus / com diu la gent / se fan hunguent / he bruxes tornen / en la nit bornen / moltes s'apleguen / de Déu reneguen / hun boch adoren / totes honoren / la llur caverna / qui·s diu Biterna / mengen e beven / aprés se lleven / per l'ayre volen / entren hon volen / sens obrir portes / moltes n·an mortes / en foch cremades / sentençiades / ab bons proçessos, / per tals exçessos / en Catalunya*»; Pau CASTELL, « "Wine vat witches...", *op. cit.*, pp. 179–180. While I was writing this book, Pau Castell informed me that he had just found several accounting records in Valencia, dated to 1428, concerning men and women accused of "being of the *boch de Biterna*" (*"ésser del boch de Biterna"*); the records also mention "a devilish demon called the *boch de Biterna*" and say that following it is a "great offense to the divine majesty" ("[...] *participants del leig, orrible e abovinable crim e de gran offensa a la maiestat divinal, del engüent d'un demoni endiablat apellat lo boch de Biterna* [...]"); Castell himself will shortly publish more details about these documents.

North of the Pyrenees, the *Boc de Biterna* appears again in the proceedings against several women from Millau and Mirepoix carried out in Toulouse in 1447. In one of them, it is stated that the accused "was the mistress of making the poisons of the entire country, of the *bouc de biterne* and of all the other evils that *sorcieres* do"[89]; in another, the *Boc* is described as a devil (*"diabolus le bouc de Bitern"*).[90]

Around 1458, the Franciscan Alonso de Espina finished writing his treatise *Fortalitium fidei*. There, we find a chapter dedicated to the *"xurguine"* or *"bruxe"*.[91] The term *"xurguine"* refers to the Basque *"sorgina"* ('sorceress' or 'witch'), a word already documented in the thirteenth century in the toponym *Sorguinariçaga* ('Oak grove of the *Sorgina*' or '*Sorginas*').[92] At the end of this chapter of Espina's book, we read:

> These perverse women abound too much in Dauphiny and in *Vaschonia*, where together at night they congregate on a deserted plain, where there is a devil [*aper*] on a rock, which they vulgarly call the *boch de Biterne*, and there they convene with lighted candles and worship the said devil kissing him on his anus. For which reason many of them [were] seized by the inquisitors of the faith and, convicted, burnt at the stake. In the seat of the inquisitor of Toulouse there are images of these [women who have been] burnt (namely, worshipping with candles the aforesaid devil) painted

---

[89] «*Estoit la maistresse de faire les poisons de tout le pais, et du bouc de Biterne, et de toutes les autres meschanteries que font les sorcieres*»; Pau CASTELL, *Orígens i evolució...*, op. cit., p. 80.

[90] «*Quod non curabat ire ad ecclesiam, quia ita promiserat Diabolo et abnegaverant Deum et fidem christianam; et quando tales se constituunt in factum hereticalibus, quidem diabolus le bouc de Bitern dat eius unum modicum diabolum qui eos regit ut dicitur*»; *ibidem*; see also Nicolas GERSHI, «Poisons, sorcières et lande de bouc», *Cahiers de recherches médiévales et humanistes*, no. 17, 2009, pp. 103–120 and Jacques FRAYSSENGE, «Le sabbat des sorcières. La répression de l'hérésie à Millau au XVe siècle», *Heresis*, no. 44–45, pp. 189–206.

[91] Joseph HANSEN, *Quellen und Untersuchungen zur Geschichte des Hexenwahns und der Hexenverfolgung im Mittelalter*, Bonn, Carl Georgi, 1901, pp. 147–148.

[92] M.ª Isabel OSTOLAZA, *Colección Diplomática de Santa María de Rocesvalles (1127–1300)*, Pamplona, Institución Príncipe de Viana, 1978, pp. 237–238, 267–268, 276–277, 396–401.

in a great number of penitential garments [*camisearum*], having seen them with my own eyes.[93]

Although "*aper*" in Latin means 'wild boar', I am inclined to accept the interpretation proposed by Pau Castell, according to which Espina would use "*aper*" in the sense of 'devil' or 'fierce leader'. Castell relies on the glossary of Du Cange, who gives the definition following the eleventh-century lexicographer Papias the Lombard.[94] Still, the closeness of the words "*aper*" and "*aquer*" is surprising.

On the other hand, it can be assumed that the "inquisitor of Toulouse" referred to in the text is Hugo Nigri, confirmed by Pope Nicholas V as inquisitor "of the Kingdom of France, the Duchy of Aquitaine, the Occitan regions and the whole of *Vasconia*" in a bull dated 1 August 1451[95]; in the fifteenth century, the term "*Vasconia*", which also features in the quoted passage from the *Fortalitium fidei*, could refer either to the Basque lands north of the Pyrenees or to the wider territory of Gascony.

Between 1471 and 1473, several witchcraft trials took place in Andorra, two of which have already been mentioned in the section on poisoned apples.[96] In several of these trials, the *Boc de Biterna* is assimilated with the Devil. One of the defendants described him as "a very big man called the Devil, almost half a man" and several of them confessed that the *Boc* had sexual intercourse with the women who attended the meetings and gave them "five sous".[97] It should be noted that in the first

---

[93] «*Nimium abundant tales perverse mulieres in Delphinatu et in Vaschonia, ubi se asserunt concurrere de nocte in quadam planicie deserta ubi est aper quidam in rupe, qui vulgariter dicitur el boch de Biterne, et quod ibi conveniunt cum candelis accensis et adorant illum aprum osculantes eum in ano suo. Ideo capte plures earum ab inquisitoribus fidei et convicte, ignibus comburuntur. Signa autem combustarum sunt depicta, qualiter scilicet adorant cum candelis predictum aprum, in domo inquisitoris Tholosani in magna multitudine camisearum, sicut ego propriis oculis aspexi*»; Joseph HANSEN, *Quellen und Untersuchungen...*, op. cit., p. 148.

[94] «*Aper significat diabolum vel ducem ferum*»; Pau CASTELL, *Orígens i evolució...*, op. cit., p. 81.

[95] «*Hugoni Nigro [...] inquisitoribus heretice pravitatis in toto Regno Francie, Ducatu Aquitaniae, Occitanisque partibus, & tota Vasconia*»; Tomás RIPOLL, *Bullarium ordinis ff. praedicatorum*, vol. III, Rome, Mainardi, 1731, p. 301.

[96] Pau CASTELL, *Orígens i evolució...*, op. cit., pp. 364–425.

[97] «*E dix més que la dita na Garreta l'a feta anar al boch de Biterna, car la dita Garreta li pasà la mà per les exelles e la untà. E li dix que digés "puya fulla". E axí se trobà de continent ab la dita Garreta defora. E axí anaren en l'ayre en una muntanya*

case, the accused claimed that, after applying an ointment on the palms of their hands and saying "*pich sobre fulla*" ('foot on leaf'), the Devil took them to "the borders of the Béarn".[98]

By the end of the fifteenth century, the *Lane de Boc* features as the place where the *Boc de Biterna* was worshipped.

In 1484, the secular justice of Pont de Suert (Lleida) prosecuted a woman named Valentina Guarner. In her statement, transcribed by the philologist Maria Dolors Farreny, we read that the accused and two companions, after having applied an ointment on the armpits and the perineum, pronounced the formula *"Pich sobre fulla e·que vaja allà on me vulla"* ('Foot on leaf and may I go wherever I please'), put "the foot on the crane", got out "through the chimney" and went to the "*lana de boch*" (this is the first mention of the *Lane de Boc* in relation to witchcraft found outside Lower Navarre). Afterwards, Valentina testified that in "the cave of the *boch*, where there is a rock", they saw a "ghost" or spirit, and that "they could hardly tell wether it was a person or a ghost". Later, among many other confessions, including the kiss on the backside, the accused stated that the "*boch de Biterna*" gave her "five sous".[99]

---

que no li recorde. E que y vehé un hom molt gran appellat lo Diable, quasi mix hom. He vehé que y eren entorn XX entre homens he dones. E los uns balaven, los altres menjaven fruyta. He ella deposant stave vergonyossa, que les altres la convidaven. E dix que lo Diable los dix: "D'on sou vengudes?". E lavos lo dit Diable pres a ella deposant. E la dita Garreta li dix que li bessàs la mà. E lavos ela li bessà la mà. E lo dit Diable: "Staràs ab mi bona anfanta?", e ella deposant li respòs que hoc. He lavós creu que li besà lo cul he li prestà homenatge e·l pres per senyor, e renegà lo Crehador. E li promés que tota hora que pogera fer mal lo fera, e que aquel mal no confesare e que rebere cascun any Nostre Senyor. E así dix interrogada que aprés usà ab ela deposant carnalment. E dix interrogada que tenie lo membre molt fret. E aprés se'n vingeren a casa»; ibid., pp. 389–390.

[98] «*E dix que ab untet que li avie donta da Roya, que al vespre se untàs los palmels de les mans, la cara e lo ventre. Interrogada si li dix de què havie fet lo dit untet. E dix que no sab. Interrogada quinyes paraules hi va dir al vespre ella deposant untant-se. E dix que "pich sobre fulla". E así ensemps ab da Roya, partint de sa casa e exint per la porta trobaren lo diable a la porta, e así en l'ayre les se'n va amenar en les fronteres de Béarn. E com foren alà se trobaren X [sic] e balaren. He lo dit boch va-li dir que li besàs la mà e li fés homenatge besàl-li lo cul, dient-li que renegàs lo Creador e "preneu a mi per senyor". [...] Interrogada si lo dit boch la strenà. E dix que hoc, que cada vegada li dave V sous»*; ibid., p. 387.

[99] «*E así diu que o·ffui. E·lavòs dix lo dit Cavaller e·lo dit Pere: "ara no·us senyàsseu per·la vida ni no nomenàsseu lo·nom de Jhesús!; e untau·vos ab aquest engüent les exelles e lo petenill", [...] "ara digau así com nosaltresdirem, pich sobre fulla e·que baja allà on me vulla!"; e diu que quiscú posà lo peu en·lo cremall. E así diu que isqueren promptament tots per·lo funeral e tiraren la volta de lana de boch. [...] E así tots en·companyia anaren-se·n*

In 1498, the Inquisition of the Catholic Monarchs prosecuted a woman called Narbona d'Arcal in Zaragoza (Aragon). The public prosecutor accused the woman of being a "*bruxa* [witch], *pozonyera* [poisoner], *nigromanta* [necromancer] and *fetillera* [sorceress]", adding:

> The said denounced prisoner, using the said witchcraft, has killed many children. And together with other women she anointed herself with certain ointments and poisons on certain parts of her person, and after anointing herself and invoking the devil and having said these words: "*Sobre arto y sobre espina al anna* [sic] *de boch vamos ayna*" ['Above shrub and above thorn to the *lanna de boch* may we go quickly'][100] the devil, in the form of a buck goat, took them to the said field of the *lanna de boch*, where the *boch de Biterna* was, whom they all kissed on his behind and honoured and worshipped him and he lay down with them and used them for the first time and gave them certain money in payment and she danced and frolicked there in the said field with many other witches until they returned to their houses, and all this at night.[101]

Last, in 1548, the Bishop of Huesca (Aragon) prosecuted a man named Jimeno de Viu. In the proceedings, we read that after having anointed himself with certain oinments:

---

en·la dita cua de·boch hon ha hun torm. E meteren-se entorn hun poch engir del dit torm. E viren aquí una fantasma, quasi no podien conéxer si·ere persona ho fantasma segons lur semblants. [...] Interrogada la dita na Valentina ella si ere bruxa, e respòs e·dix que hoc. Interrogada [...]. E lavòs ella li prestà la mà al·dit boch de Biterna, [...]. E dix que lavòs que en·senyal de homenatge ella lo besà en·lo cul. E·lo dit boch de Biterna donà cinch sous a son cosingermà»; Maria Dolors FARRENY, *Processos de crims del segle XV a Lleida. Transcripció i estudi lingüístic*, Lleida, Institut d'Estudis Ilerdencs, 1986, pp. 102–103.

[100] Several Basque folk narratives record a similar formula: "*Sasi guztien gainetik, laino guztien azpitik*" ('Above all the brambles, beneath all the clouds'); José Miguel de BARANDIARÁN, *Brujería y brujas...*, *op. cit.*, pp. 91–102.

[101] «*La dicha rea denunciada, usando del dicho officio de bruxa, ha matado muchas criaturas. Y se untava con otras con ciertos untos y pozonyas en ciertas partes de su persona, y aprés de untada y de invocado al demonio y de haver dicho estas palabras: «Sobre arto y sobre espina al anna* [sic] *de boch vamos ayna». Y dicho esto, las tomava el diablo en forma de cabrón y las llevava al dicho campo del anna de boch, en donde estaba el boch de Biterna, al qual todas besavan en el trasero y lo honrravan y adoravan y se echava con ellas y las estrenava y les dava en pago ciertos dineros y bailava y se zolazava allí en el dicho campo con otras muchas bruxas ata que se tornavan a sus casas, y esto todo de noche*»; Carmen ESPADA, *La vieja Narbona. De las sombras del alba, al resplandor de las hogueras*, Zaragoza, Certeza Libros, 1998, pp. 174, 176 and 181.

He said three times: *"Sobre arto y sobre spina al alna* [sic] *de boch seamos ayna"*, and went out of his house [...], and met a devil in the shape of a black man, who led him and guided him to the *alna de boch*, which is in Gascony, where he met other men and women dancing to the sound of a fiddle around a great stone, on top of which was on feet the *buch de Biterna*, who had goat feet and was black.[102]

12   May de Biterna

The next group of evidence (three poems) will take us to the Lectoure region in Armagnac (Gascony).

In the proceedings against Valentina Guarner, we have already seen the magic formula *"Pich sobre fulla e·que vaja allà on me vulla"* ('Foot on leaf and may I go wherever I please'), while an abbreviated version (*"Pich sobre fulla"*) appeared in one of the Andorran processes from 1471.[103] Although he did not quote these early testimonies, the historian Jean Pierre Piniès published in 2006 an interesting article containing numerous variants of this formula.[104] Among them, a brief mention from 1620 by the poet André Du Pré, born in Lectoure, stands out because it links it to spiritual journeys:

The *haitilleres* go wherever they want by fantasy / when, anointed with unguents, the soul departs from their bodies, / saying *pic sur houeille*,

---

[102] «*Con otros bruxones y bruxas y mallefficos, sus cómplices y sequaçes, se untó con ciertos untos, es a saber, de polbos y çumo de sapos, y de arsenich, y de otras ponçonyas, mezclados con verbena y con otras yerbas, las palmas de las manos y las plantas de los pies, y debaxo de los sobacos y los pechos en drecho del coraçón, y assí untado dixo por tres vezes: «Sobre arto y sobre spina al alna* [sic] *de boch seamos ayna», y salió de su casa fuera de dicho lugar, y falló un diablo en figura de hombre negro, el cual le llevó y guió hasta el alna de boch, que es en Gascunya, donde falló otros hombres y mugeres baylando al son de un rabiquete en derredor de hun gran canto, encima del qual estaba en pies el buch de Biterna, que tenía los pies de cabra y era negro*»; María TAUSIET, *Ponzoña en los ojos. Brujería y superstición en Aragón en el siglo XVI*, Zaragoza, Institución «Fernando el Católico», 2000, pp. 281 and 285. For other sixteenth century sources on the *Boc de Biterna*, see Pau CASTELL, *Orígens i evolució...*, *op. cit.*, pp. 77–83, Ángel GARI, «Brujería en los Pirineos (siglos XIII al XVII). Aproximación a su historia», *Cuadernos de Etnología y Etnografía de Navarra*, no. 85, 2010, pp. 330–333 and Carlos GARCÉS, *La mala semilla. Nuevos casos de brujas*, Barcelona, Tropo, 2013, pp. 115 and 150.

[103] See nn. 98 and 99 above.

[104] Jean Pierre PINIÈS, «*Pet-sus-fuèlha* ou le départ des sorcières pour le sabbat», *Heresis*, no. 44–45, 2006, pp. 247–266.

and up the crane / they leave the body, they go wherever sin commands them.[105]

The similarity between this last phrase and the line "as destiny commands them" from the *Roman de la Rose*[106] implies that we should not exclude a possible learned inspiration, at least partial, in Du Pré's poem. Nevertheless, more than 50 years earlier, in 1567, Pey de Garros—also born in Lectoure—had already mentioned the *Lane de Boc*, and linked it with animal metamorphosis:

> You have told us of true *brolhariâs* [probably from "*bro*" or "*broèle*"; 'broth' and 'mush' respectively] / of incantations, and of *sortilhariâs*. / You could die if in the *lana de boc* / you have not been, if any man has ever been there, / and if you have not frolicked with the *hantaumas* [ghosts, witches?], / who become cats, now pigs, maybe asses.[107]

Finally, in the most surprising of the three poems, in 1611, Jean de Garros—brother of Pey de Garros—mentioned the term "*Biterne*", but, despite the sorcerous context, he did not do so in relation to a *boc*:

> Of snakes, serpents, toads and a rotten lizard, / with which she poisons your heart, the poisoner, / *de biterne la may*, mistress sorceress.[108]

This "*may de Biterne*" likewise appears in a popular expression collected in the twentieth century—also in Armagnac —by Simin Palay:

---

[105] «*Las haitilleres ban oun bon per fantasie, / quan, untades d'engouens, l'arme deu cos lous sail / en disen pic sur houeille, et cabsus lou carmail / leichan lou cos, se'n ban oun lou peccat las mie*»; André DU PRÉ, *Pouesies gascoues (1620)*, critic edition by Joan-Francés Courouau, Montpellier, Seccion Francesa de l'Associacion Internacionau d'Estudis Occitans, 1995, p. 55.

[106] See n. 36 above.

[107] «*Tu nos as dit de berâs brolhariâs, / d'encantamens, e de sortilhariâs / Poscas mouri si en lana de boc / tu n'es estât, si james home y hoc, / e si tu n'as trepât dam las hantaumas, / qui se hen gatz, ara porcz, tantos saumas*»; Pey de GARROS, *Poesias gasconas*, Toulouse, Jammes Colomes, 1567, p. 50.

[108] «*De serps, serpents, grapauts & d'un lausert poirit, / don ere empousouéc, ton co la pousouére, / de biterne la may, mastresse surtilhére*»; Jean de GARROS, *Pastourade gascoue sur la mort deu magnific é pouderous Anric quart deu nom rey de France é de Navarre*, Toulouse, Jean Boude, 1611, p. 15.

"*La may de Biterne te brùlle!*" ('May the *may de Biterne* burn you!').[109] "*May*", "*mair*" or "*maire*" means 'mother' in Occitan. In this sense, in the French glossary at the end of his book, Jean de Garros explains that "the *may de Biterne* is taken for the mother of hells".[110] Yet, these are, as far as I know, the only two sources that speak of this figure, at least under this name.

13 THE MOTHER OF GOD

Back in the early fourteenth century, we find an account concerning another "mother" in which several already familiar elements are mixed with features of Cathar origin. A woman from Gourdon-en-Quercy—accused of making potions for love and peace, invoking demons and practising divination by melting lead—confessed in 1317:

> In the last 15 years, a great number of times she has been dead and has gone to the other century [the other world], to the *Nairo* [sic] meadow [*prat*]; and in that meadow there are a great number of apple trees and fountains; in that meadow, the mother [*maire*] of God is sitting on a chair [or throne], and three virgins beside her; and she has seen that the souls passed from this century to the other came to worship the mother of God, and [they] also [went] to [other] eight places, and then they came to the *repaus* [paradisiacal place in which, according to the Cathars, after doing penance in various churches and places, the souls rest while waiting for the Day of Judgment]; those souls had their bodies, as here [in this century, in this world]; and she has recognized a great number of Gourdon, whom she named; and when she had been there a long time, she would come back. And past that meadow there was a river in which a great number of women washed the cloths they had stolen here, and they will wash them until the Day of Judgment.[111]

---

[109] Simin PALAY, *Dictionnaire du béarnais...*, *op. cit.*, vol. II, p. 650.

[110] «*La may de Biterne est prise pour la mère des enfers*»; Jean de GARROS, *Pastourade gascoue...*, *op. cit.*, p. 37.

[111] «*E may dih que de XV ans ensai gran re de vet es estada morta e es anada e l'autre setgle ensaiquas que al prat Nairo, e en aquel pratz a gran re pomies e fons, en aquel Prat es la maire de Dio que sese en una cadera, e III vergenas latz, e las armas pasadas d'aquest setgle a l'autre vit que venian aorar la maire de Dio, e mai en VIII locz, e poi venian en repaus, las quals armas avian lor cors, coma say. E conog ni gran re de Gordo, lasquals nomnet, et quant avia aqui gran temps estat ela s'en tornava. E pasat aquel prat avia I rio el qual gran re de femnas lavavo bugada els draps que avian say panatz,*

The German theologian Johannes Nider (1380–1438) mentioned in his *Preceptorium divine legis* certain women who "claim that, on Ember Days [*in quatuor temporibus*], in ecstasy, they see the souls in purgatory and many other phantoms".[112] This passage was literally quoted by Martin de Arles (around 1495) few lines after stating the already mentioned abundance "in the Basque [*basconica*] region north of the Pyrenees" of women who believed that rode at night with "Diana, goddess of pagans", and that "transformed themselves into other creatures".[113]

In fact, without leaving the Gascon area, we will now approach the vicinity of the Kingdom of Navarre in order to find a third "mother".

14 THE DEVILESS

Although it is likely that the denunciations made by Johannette de Sala in 1450 exacerbated repression and provoked new judicial processes, I have already commented in Sect. 10 above that no other fifteenth-century sources survive regarding sorcery or witchcraft in Lower Navarre (with the exception of the passages in Martin de Arles' treatise and the references to "*xurguine*" and "*Vaschonia*" by Alonso de Espina). Yet, the historian François Bordes showed that there are references pointing to the existence of witch-hunts in the neighbouring regions of Chalosse and Marensin between the 1440s and 1460s.[114]

---

e lavaran ensaiquas que al dia de Jutgamen»; Archives municipales de Gourdon, FF II, f. 123v; transcription in Annie CHARNAY, «Criminalité et superstition à Gourdon-en-Quercy au début du XIVe siècle. L'histoire d'une sorcière» in *Mélanges historiques midi-pyrénéens*, Toulouse, Les Amis des Archives de la Haute-Garonne, 1992, p. 86. I am grateful to Delphine Soubiroux-Magrez, the association Héritages du Sénéchal and the Municipality of Gourdon for providing me with reproductions of the sorcery trials kept in their fourteenth-century records.

[112] «[...] *in quatuor temporibus se in raptu dicunt videre animas purgatorii et plura alia fantasmata*»; Johannes NIDER, *Preceptorium divine legis*, Paris, André Bocard, 1531, preceptum primum, cap. X, f. 25; see also Carlo GINZBURG, *Los benandanti*, Guadalajara (Jalisco), Universidad de Guadalajara, 2005, chap. 2, sections 5–6, pp. 73–77.

[113] José GOÑI, «El tratado *De Superstitionibus*...», *op. cit.*, pp. 276–278; see also note 27 above.

[114] François BORDES, *Sorciers et sorcieres: Procès de sorcellerie en Gascogne et Pays Basque*, Toulouse, Éditions Privat, 1999, pp. 21–22.

For example, thanks to a jurisdictional enquiry from 1501, we know that, during the English occupation of the territory, i.e. before 1450, Archambault de Caupenne had at least two groups of women condemned as "*sorcieres*" and burnt in Amou (seven or eight the first time and three the second time). Shortly afterwards, the same Archambault ordered the arrest of a third group of women, locking them up in his castle. However, these were released when French troops reconquered the territory in 1451. Coincidentally—or perhaps not—it is in Amou, 40 km north of Ilharre, where we can find a new testimony about the *Lane de Boc*, in the sixteenth century.

In the 1613 edition of his *Tableau de l'inconstance*, the magistrate Pierre de Lancre summarised, translated from Gascon into French and probably polished the declaration made by Estebene de Cambrue, parishioner of Amou, aged 25, on the 18th December 1567:

> She says that the Witches go to the great assembly and to the great Sabbath only four times a year, in derision of the ceremonies which the Church celebrates on the four annual feasts. The small assemblies which are held near towns or parishes, where only those of the place attend, they call them *esbats*; and they are held now in one place of the said parish, now in another, where one does nothing but jump and frolic [*folastrer*], the Devil not being there with all his great array as at the great assemblies. The place of this great convocation is generally called all over the country the *Lanne de Bouc*, where they dance around a stone, which is standing in the said place, on which sits a big black man, whom they call *Monsieur*, and each of the assembly goes to kiss his behind, and they are carried to the said place, on a beast, which sometimes seems a horse, and sometimes a man.[115]

---

[115] «*Estebene de Cambrue aagee de 25 ans de la parroisse d'Amou [...] dit que les Sorcieres n'alloient en la grande assemblee & au grand Sabbat que quatre fois l'annee, en derision des ceremonies que l'Eglise celebre les quatre festes annuelles. Car les petites assemblees qui se font pres des villes ou parroisses, où il n'y va que ceux du lieu, ils les appellent les esbats; & se font ores en un lieu de ladite parroisse, ores en un autre, où on ne faict que sauter & folastrer, le Diable n'y estant avec tout son grand arroy comme aux grandes assemblees. Que le lieu de ceste grande convocation, s'appelle generalement par tout le pays la Lanne de Bouc. Où ils se mettent à dancer à l'entour d'une pierre, qui est plantee audit lieu, sur laquelle est assis un grand homme noir, qu'elles appellent Monsieur, & chacun de l'assemblee luy va baiser le derriere, & se font porter iusqu'audit lieu, sur une beste, qui semble par fois un cheval, & parfoys un homme*»; Pierre de LANCRE, *Tableau de l'inconstance..., op. cit.*, p. 123.

A few lines below, the text reproduces, in Gascon, the formula that witches pronounce "when they are going a long way" (a variant of those seen above): "*Pic suber hoeilhe, enta la lanne de bouc bien m'arrecoueille*" ('Foot on leaf, may the *lanne de bouc* welcome me').[116] Finally, we read that:

> There [in the *Lanne de Bouc*, in the Sabbath], they disown God, the Virgin Mary and the rest, and take Satan as their father and protector, and the *Diablesse* [Deviless] as their mother.[117]

If this passage really was part of the declaration made by Estebene de Cambrue in 1567, this would be the first of only three known sources from the Pyrenees about a supernatural female figure co-presiding over the witches' meetings. The second one will be discussed in the following section, while the third—transcribed below—remains problematic because it reproduces a formulation very similar to that of De Lancre's text; it is a document from the inquisitors of Barcelona about the case against Joan de Mollera (1620), previously tried by the secular justice in Castelldefels:

> The said women and the defendant said [that] in many of the said meetings they took the devil as their father, and the *diablessa* as their mother.[118]

15 AQUERLARRE

Around the year 1340, the Portuguese Pedro Afonso, Count of Barcelos, retold a Melusinian legend in which Diego Lopez, Lord of Biscay, married a "very beautiful and very well dressed" woman he found singing "on the top of a stone" during a shoot in the mountains. According to

---

[116] «*Et quand ils font un long chemin, ils disent tels mots;* Pic suber hoeilhe, enta la lanne de bouc bien m'arrecoueille»; *ibidem*.

[117] «*Là ils renient Dieu, la Vierge & le reste, & prennent Satan pour leur pere & protecteur, & la Diablesse pour leur mere*»; *ibidem*.

[118] «*Las dichas mugeres y el reo dezían en muchas de las dichas juntas que tomavan al diablo por padre, y a la diablassa por madre*»; AHN (Archivo Histórico Nacional), Inq., Lib. 732, f. 492v. I am grateful to Pau Castell for informing me of the existence of this document and providing me with the transcription of the passage.

Barcelos' account, the lady had a "goat foot".[119] In addition, Basque folklore abounds with stories about female figures—probably local variants of the same numen—who are usually called "Señora" ('Mistress'), "Dama" ('Lady'), "Mari" or "Maya". According to the legends, they live in the caves of the great peaks of the Basque orography, such as Anboto, Aizkorri or Aralar.[120] The following account is set in the Araitz Valley (Upper Navarre), in the shadow of the Aralar mountain range (where the toponym *Aker çaltua* was located in the eleventh century).[121]

In early 1595, Maria Miguel de Orexa, parishioner of the small village of Intza, was publicly identified as a witch [*bruxa*] by a witch finder. The young Johana de Baraibar y Arangoa, aged 12 and resident in the nearby village of Baraibar, claimed to be able to recognise witches by a mark they had in their eyes. According to the young girl, the mark appeared after having attended the witches' meeting just once, and did not disappear even if the person confessed that sin. Having been identified by Johana, "and seeing the girl told the truth", Maria Miguel de Orexa went to the palace of Andueza, the residence of Fermin de Lodosa, Lord of Andueza and Perpetual Mayor of the Araitz Valley, to make a statement.[122]

The identification of Maria Miguel was followed by others, and within a few days a total of 11 residents of Intza were arrested by the Lord of Andueza. Later, the detainees—including Maria Miguel—were sent to Pamplona, where they were to be tried by the Tribunal de la Corte

---

[119] «*Este dom Diego Lopez era mui boo monteiro, e estando ũu dia em sa armada atendendo quando verria o porco, ouvio cantar muita alta voz ũa molher em cima de ũa pena. E el foi pera la e vio-a ser mui fermosa e mui bem vistida; [...] e esta dona era mui fermosa e mui bem feita em todo seu corpo, salvando que havia ũu pee forçado como pee de cabra [...]*»; Juan PAREDES, *Las narraciones de los* Livros de linhagens, Granada, Universidad de Granada, 1995, p. 194.

[120] José Miguel de BARANDIARÁN, *Diccionario ilustrado de mitología vasca*, Bilbao, Editorial La Gran Enciclopedia Vasca, 1972, pp. 157–168.

[121] See n. 61 above.

[122] «*[...] a ocassión de una mochacha que los días passados llegó en el dicho lugar [de Inza], llamada Juana de Varevar, natural del lugar de Varevar, a reconocer los brujos que en él havía; y entre otras que conosció en el dicho lugar fue una de ellas esta que declara, deziendo que se le echaba de ver que lo era por tener en los ojos rastro de sapos, y como vio que en ello dezía la verdad, acudió ante el dicho don Fermín de Lodossa y asecretó su deposición*»; AGN, Tribunales Reales, Procesos, no. 071319, f. 49r.

(civil justice). The investigations continued and, between April and May 1595, the number of people under arrest (mostly women) rose to 17. The proceedings dragged on, and by June eight of the imprisoned women had died, probably victims of hunger and disease caused by the insalubrious conditions in the prison in Pamplona; Maria Miguel de Orexa was one of those who died. The trial culminated in November with just one conviction: Martin de Barazarte was condemned to one hundred lashes and banishment from the kingdom for six years.[123]

The document that records the deposition of Maria Miguel de Orexa before the Lord of Andueza indicates that the interrogation began on Wednesday 1st February 1595 and lasted until four o'clock in the afternoon on the following day.[124] Although the report is written in Spanish, thanks to the account of her second deposition—made before the magistrates of the court in Pamplona—we know that Maria Miguel did not speak Spanish, so her declarations before the Lord of Andueza had to be made in Basque and subsequently, or simultaneously, translated and transcribed into Spanish by the notary Juan de Areso; nevertheless, Maria Miguel ratified in Pamplona what she had previously said in the palace of Andueza.[125]

Let us focus now on the content of the transcript of that first statement:

> Maria Miguel de Orexa [...] aged twenty-six or so [...] said that when she was about ten years old, Maria de Chiqui Balda, grandmother of this

---

[123] Florencio IDOATE, *La brujería en Navarra...*, *op. cit.*, pp. 131–143, 159–161, 354–371, 375–377; Florencio IDOATE, «Los brujos del Valle de Araiz» in *Brujología. Congreso de San Sebastián. Ponencias y comunicaciones*, Madrid, Seminarios y Ediciones S.A., 1975, pp. 53–68.

[124] AGN, Tribunales Reales, Procesos, no. 071319, ff. 1r-6r. Florecio Idoate partially transcribed the statement of Maria Miguel de Orexa in Florencio IDOATE, *El señorío de Sarría*, Pamplona, Gráficas Iruña, 1959, pp. 627–629. However, he did not transcribe the oldest version (the one used here), but a later copy also included in the process preserved in the AGN. Among the papers in the file, there are copies of all the statements, probably copied to be sent to the Spanish Inquisition and later returned. The Inquisition did not intervene in the process.

[125] «[...] *pidió se le leyesse [su deposición], y por mandado de los dichos señores alcaldes, yo el predicho secretario le leí aquella desde su principio asta el fin, que es la depossición del primer testimonio; y después que se le dio a entender lo contenido en ella palabra por palabra en su lengua vascongada, dixo que aquella era su deposición y lo que dixo y depusso ante el dicho don Fermín de Lodossa y Andueça por presencia del dicho Juan de Aresso y que lo ratificaba y ratificó*»; AGN, Tribunales Reales, Procesos, no. 071319, f. 49r.

deponent, being at the time of her death, called her and told her that this declarant should take charge of the office of witch that she had done in her time, and she answered her that she would in no way do or take charge of the said office, and that she should command her something else, and the said grandmother replied that she had to take charge of the said office because otherwise her soul could not be torn out of her; and that this declarant should at least go to the field where the witches hold their meeting, and that she would have company for it; to which she replied that even if she went to the said field (the said grandmother did not specify to her which the said field was, but only that the companions would show her), that on the part of this declarant they would see that it was not her will to take up the said office of witch; and on the night when the aforementioned happened, the said Marichiqui Balda, her grandmother, passed away.[126]

The following night, while Maria Miguel "was in her parents' house, in bed", a neighbour, her aunt and her father came to her, applied an ointment on her head and, all of them wearing "white shirts", took her

---

[126] «María Miguel de Orexa [...] de veinte y seis años poco más o menos [...] dixo que siendo esta que declara de edad de diez años poco más o menos, María de chiqui Balda, agüela desta que depone, estando a la ora de su muerte, le llamó y le dixo que esta que declara se abía de encargar del oficio de bruxa que ella en su tiempo abía echo, y esta le respondió que de ninguna manera aría ni se encargaría del dicho oficio y que le mandasse en otra cossa, y la dicha su agüela le tornó a replicar que ella se abía de encargar del dicho su oficio porque de otra manera no se le podía rancar la alma; y que a lo menos abía de yr esta que declara al campo donde las brujas azen su junta, y que ya tendría compañía para ello; a lo qual le respondió que aunque fuesse al dicho campo, que no le especificó la dicha su agüela quál hera el dicho campo, sino tan solamente que le enseñarían los compañeros, que por esta que declara berían no hera su voluntad de azer el dicho oficio de bruja; y en la noche que passó lo susodicho feneció sus días la dicha Marichiqui Balda, su agüela», ibid., f. 1; in order to make the transcript easier to read, I have added punctuation marks, capital letters and accents.

"in the air" to the slope of Urriçola, next to Intza. There they met 15 other residents of the village.[127]

References to going to the meetings wearing "white shirts" or linens—the clothes they slept in—appear numerous times in the documentation relating to a series of trials and enquiries from 1575 and 1576 in Upper Navarre. For example, one of the accused in Anotzibar confessed that a devil "used to make her get out of bed in her shirt" to take her to the gathering.[128]

Returning to Maria Miguel de Orexa's statement:

> And from the said slope, all together and in the air, they came to a plain that she who declares does not know where it is, nor could she find it during the day but at night at the time she usually goes to the afore-mentioned meeting; and on arriving there they found a large number of witches who were dancing with the same outfit as this declarant and her said companions; that the said outfit were white shirts; she did not know any of those they found in the said field, because they were from other parties outside the Arayz Valley; but that some were men and others women, as could be seen in their physiognomies; and in the middle of the said field, on two chairs that looked like gold, were two black figures [*bultos negros*], one of which looked like a man with two horns on his head in the manner of a *cabrón* [buck goat], and the other figure looked like a woman. And these figures were dressed in white; and when she and her said companions arrived, they also began to dance together with the others, in the presence of the said figures; [...] and after they had danced for a while, they all followed the said figures, this declarant and all the others in the air, to a cave that is near the said plain; and in it they usually

---

[127] «*Y la otra noche siguiente a prima noche, estando esta que declara en cassa de sus dichos padres y en la cama, llegaron en ella Gracia de Pelejero o Çamarguinarena y Gracia de Orexa, hija de la sobredicha Marichiqui Balda agüela desta que declara y hermana de Miguel de Orexa, su padre; todos los quales juntamente con el dicho su padre, le untaron en la cabeça con una cosa que parecía aceite y a manera de ungüento, no se acuerda la color que tenía, y al mismo instante salieron todos juntos, y en el ayre dieron en la cuesta que llaman Urriçola, que está en la dicha valle y junto al lugar de Inça, donde allaron estando en pie y con sus camissas blancas, con el qual ábito yban esta que declara y sus dichos compañeros; y los que assí allaron en la dicha cuesta de Urriçola son* [the document names 15 residents of Intza]»; *ibid.*, ff. 1v-2r.

[128] Florencio IDOATE, *La brujería en Navarra...*, *op. cit.*, pp. 307, 309, 315 and 320.

worship [the figures] on their backside, namely the women worship the aforementioned figure that looks like a man, and the men worship the one that looks like a woman.[129]

The said figures then had sexual intercourse with the attendants, the male figure with the women and the female one with the men. Once the male was finished, he gave the women some money, but Maria Miguel did not know if the female figure did the same with the men.[130] Next:

> They leave in the air, each one to their lands and houses; and the said return they usually make and it is good for them to do so before the roosters crow because they usually talk among themselves and they have it as a rule that if they did not return before the roosters crow, they would not afterwards have the power they had before; although this one deponent has not found herself in this danger.[131]

---

[129] «Y desde la dicha cuesta, todos juntos y en el ayre, dieron en un llano que esta que declara no sabe dónde es ni podría allar de día sino de noches al tiempo que suele yr a la sobredicha junta; mas de que en llegando en él allaron mucho número de bruxas que andaban dançando con el propio ábito que esta que declara y sus dichos compañeros; que el dicho ábito eran sendas camisas blancas; no conoçió entre los que assí allaron en el dicho campo a nenguno, por ser de otras partidas fuera de la Valle de Arayz; mas de que los unos heran hombres y otras mugeres, según se les echaba de ber en sus fisonomías; y en medio del dicho campo, en sendas sillas que pareçían de oro, dos bultos negros, que el uno pareçía ser hombre con dos cuernos en la cabeça a manera de cabrón, y el otro bulto pareçía que era muger. Y estos bultos estaban bestidos de blanco; y luego que assí llegaron esta que declara y sus dichos compañeros, también principiaron a dançar juntamente con los demás, en presencia de los sobredichos bultos; y la música que tenían hera de tambolines, atabal y rabel; y de los músicos solo conoçió a los dichos Micheto de Usar y su hijo Juanes, el mayor, que tiene el pescueço tuerto, y el padre tocaba el atabal y el hijo el rabel; y a cabo de un rato que assí dançaron, fueron todos tras los dichos bultos, esta que declara y todos los demas en el ayre a una cueba que está cerca del dicho llano; y en ella suelen adorar en el trassero a saber las mugeres al sobredicho bulto que parece hombre, y los hombres al que parece muger»; AGN, Tribunales Reales, Procesos, no. 071319, f. 2.

[130] «Y al tiempo que le adoran se ponen de rodillas, y en bessando luego, el dicho bulto de hombre abraça a las mugeres y asse su acto teniendo cópula con ellas, y los hombres que son bruxos assen lo mismo con el bulto que parece ser muger; y acabado esto les da dineros el dicho bulto de hombre a las mugeres, que el dinero que assí les da parece ser real de a quatro; no sabe declarar si el dicho bulto de muger da el dicho dinero a los hombres»; ibid., ff. 2v-3r.

[131] «Mas de que se despiden luego en el ayre cada uno a sus tierras y cassas; y la dicha vuelta suelen azer y les combiene que agan antes que canten los gallos porque entre ellos se suele platicar y tienen de horden que ssi no bolbiessen antes de cantar los gallos, no tendrían

Here, there would seem to be an interruption in the statement. The male figure on the chair also features in the documents from 1575 to 1576. The least diabolical version is found in Anotzibar in 1575, where the brothers Martin and Miguel de Olagüe—aged seven and ten respectively—stated:

> In the place where they go to the gathering, a man sitting on a chair that has no leather, but is made of wood, [...] said to this witness the first time: "You are welcome". And he says this to everyone whenever they meet. [...] And he is an old man, [...] with a long, grey beard. [...] And they kiss his hand. [...] And the said old man [...] usually plays a flute and a *mandurria*, and those who meet at the said gathering, who are many men and women, dance and rejoice to their sound.[132]

The horns on the head appeared as well in 1576, in the declaration of another ten-year-old girl, Maria de Echeandi, from the town of Ziga:

> And the two of them went together [...] to a plain that is [...] about half a league from the said place of Ciga. And in the said part they found that a large man was sitting on a chair, all dressed in gold and he had two golden horns and one could hardly recognise his face. And with him were Catalina, the widow who lives in the house of Echeverria, who said she was the queen, and Graxiana de Echenique, the young, [...].[133]

---

después la facultad que de primero; aunque esta que depone no se a visto en este peligro»; ibid., f. 3r.

[132] «*En el lugar a donde ban al maleficio, un hombre sentado en una silla que no tiene cuero, sino que es de madera, [...] le dixo en la primera vez a este testigo: "Seas bien venido". Y lo acostumbra decir a todos en las veces que se ayuntan. [...] Y este hombre es viejo, [...] con una barba larga y cana. [...] Y le besan la mano. [...] Y el dicho hombre viejo [...] suele tañer una flauta y una mandurria, y a su son dançan y se regocijan los que se ayuntan en el dicho ayuntamiento, que son muchos hombres y mujeres*»; Florencio IDOATE, *La brujería en Navarra...*, op. cit., pp. 307–313; AGN, Tribunales Reales, Procesos, no. 069853, ff. 14v-15r.

[133] «*Y así fueron las dos juntas [...] a un raso que está [...] a media legoa poco más o menos del dicho lugar de Ciga. Y en la dicha parte hallaron que estaba asentado en una silla un hombre grande, todo vestido de oro y que tenía dos cuernos de oro y casi no se le conocía la cara. Y con él estaban Catalina, la viuda que es la que vive en casa de Echeverria, que decía era la reina y Graxiana de Echenique, moza, [...]*»; AGN, Tribunales Reales, Procesos, no. 344108, ff. 1v-2r.

Finally, also in 1576, we find the nefarious kiss in the testimony of a witness from Lizaso:

> In the gatherings, they had a black man sitting on a big golden chair, and there they kissed him on his backside.[134]

However, although in some testimonies a "queen" is mentioned—as we have seen in Ziga and was also recorded in Zugarramurdi (1609–1611)[135]—the 1595 process we are dealing with here is the first and only case in the Upper Navarrese documentation where a supernatural female figure co-presided over the meeting.

The other defendants' statements confirm or reproduce Maria Miguel's account, although there are slight variations. For example, Mari Hernandoiz de Perugorri said that the man was black and the woman was beautiful and white and dressed in green, that the men kissed the latter on her face and pointed to Fridays as "the most frequent nights to go to the said field".[136] In addition, as with this last piece of information about Fridays, other suspects contributed new elements to Maria Miguel's account. This was the case of Juan Martiniz de Perugorri—uncle of the previous defendant—who, in his testimony before the court magistrates in Pamplona, briefly mentioned metamorphosis:

> He remembers having seen in the said field [...], many children of tender age, who he does not know whose they were, and it seems to him that

---

[134] «*En los ayuntamientos tenían a un ombre negro asentado en una silla grande de oro, y allí le besaban en el trasero*»; Florencio IDOATE, *La brujería en Navarra...*, op. cit., p. 342.

[135] Gustav HENNINGSEN, *El abogado de las brujas. Brujería vasca e inquisición española*, trans. by Marisa Rey-Henningsen, Madrid, Alianza Editorial, 2010, pp. 139–140.

[136] «[*Su tío*] *la puso a la dicha Mari Hernández delante de dos figuras que estaban asentadas en dos sillas como doradas y la una figura era como de un hombre negro y alzado con un sombrero y dos cuernos en la cabeza y con una cabellera larga hasta los hombros y una barba negra y vestido de paño negro con rostro, manos y pies como de hombre aunque todo era muy negro. Y la otra figura era como de mujer que estaba asentada en la dicha silla con parecer hermoso y blanco y vestida de verde con rostro, manos y pies de mujer. [...] Con el bulto de mujer los hombres que danzaban le besaban en el rostro y tenían acceso con ella. [...] y las noches que más frecuentaban a ir al dicho campo eran los viernes*»; AGN, Tribunales Reales, Procesos, no. 071319, ff. 30r-36r; Jesús María USUNÁRIZ, «La caza de brujas en la Navarra moderna (siglos XVI–XVII)», RIEV, no. 9, 2012, pp. 324–325.

they all turned into cats and dogs, and that in this figure they roamed in the said field, and afterwards returned to their initial state.[137]

Returning to Maria Miguel de Orexa's statement, if we take a closer look, her account seems to be constructed to claim that the first instance was the only time that she attended the meeting, and that there she refused to take up the "witch's office" that her grandmother had carried out. However, likely after being subjected to pressure and threats from the Lord of Andueza, when she resumed her testimony, Maria Miguel confessed to having gone "many times" to the meetings and to having had carnal relations "with the said black figure they call Bercebut".[138] Furthermore, despite having said in the first part of the deposition that "she did not know any of those they found in the said field, because they were from other parties outside the Arayz Valley", in this second part she named dozens of people from Intza and other villages in the valley whom she said she had seen at the meetings, including the priests of Arriba and Errazkin. In fact, this last point appears to have been of particular interest to her interrogators.[139]

Finally, asked about infanticides and other evildoings against "cereals and livestock or something else", Maria Miguel described how, with several companions, she had caused two mares and some sheep to fall off a cliff. In the account of the latter, we read:

> And it may be a year or so that, coming to the said land and place of Inça, from the said field of *aquer larre*, this declarant together with Gracia de Çamarguinarena and Juanes de Çamarguinarena, her son, and passing through the mountain range that they call Aralarr, they found a flock of

---

[137] «*Se acuerda haver visto en el dicho campo* [...], *muchos niños de tierna hedad, que no save cuyos eran, y le parece que todos ellos se convertían en gatos y perros, y que en esta figura andavan en el dicho campo, y que después volvían a su ser primero*»; Florencio IDOATE, «Brujerías en la montaña de navarra en el siglo XVI», *Príncipe de Viana*, no. 223, 2001, p. 320.

[138] «[...] *con el dicho bulto negro que ellos llaman Bercebut*»; AGN, Tribunales Reales, Procesos, no. 071319, f. 3r.

[139] *Ibid.*, ff. 3v-4v.

sheep [...], they followed them, and the said sheep, having gone on a rampage, many of them fell off the cliff.[140]

Although witches' meetings in different meadows and fields are present in Biscayan documentation since 1508 (Durango trials),[141] and in the Upper Navarrese one since 1525 (Ituren trials),[142] this is the oldest known reference to "*aquer larre*".[143] As we have already seen in Sect. 9, "*aquer larre*", in Basque, means exactly the same as "*lane de boc*" ('field, heath or meadow of the buck goat') and is a calque of "*boquelane*", although it is more likely that the calque was in the opposite direction.

Maria Miguel's statement mentions the "field of *aquer larre*" three times. In addition, throughout the more than 200 pages

---

[140] «*Y puede aber un año o algo menos que, beniendo assí bien para la dicha su tierra y lugar de Inça, desdel dicho campo de aquer larre, esta que declara juntamente con Gracia de Çamarguinarena y Juanes de Çamarguinarena, su hijo, y pasando por la sierra que llaman Aralarr, allaron un rabaño de obejas [...], les siguieron, y las dichas obejas, aviéndose alborotado, se despeñaron muchas dellas*»; *ibid.*, f. 5r; it should be remembered that the original document does not use capital letters at the beginning of person or place names.

[141] Eudaldo ARANDA, «La quema de brujas de 1507. Notas en torno a un enigma histórico», *Huarte de San Juan*, no. 17, 2010, pp. 420–422; Pedro FERNÁNDEZ DE VILLEGAS, *La traducción del Dante de lengua toscana en verso castellano*, Burgos, Fadrique Alemán de Basilea, 1515, f. 225; Ander BERROJALBIZ, *Los herejes de Amboto*. «*Luteranos*» *en el año 1500*, Arre, Pamiela, 2016, pp. 39–43; Ander BERROJALBIZ and Joseba SARRIONANDIA, *La hija de los herejes*, Arre, Pamiela, 2018, pp. 44–46 and 55–57; see also Darío de AREITIO, «Las brujas de Ceberio [año 1558]», RIEV, vol. 18, no. 4, pp. 654–664.

[142] Florencio IDOATE, *La brujería en Navarra...*, *op. cit.*, pp. 46–48.

[143] The researcher Juainas Paul Arzak stated in an article published in 2008 that "it appears as a place name in 1525 in Ituren, referring to a field called *aquerrlarea* [AGN, Tribunales Reales, Procesos, no. 035728]"; Juainas PAUL, «El aquelarre, una invención afortunada», *op. cit.*, p. 13. However, although he points out the process number, Paul Arzak does not indicate the folio on which the reference is found. On the other hand, and in the opposite sense, Florencio Idoate—after having analysed, in principle, the same documentation—wrote in 1978: "The word *aquelarre* or *aquerlarre* is not used in this process; the word *conventículos* [covens] appears, which according to some of the defendants, took place in Mendaurre (today Mendaur), also called Abalegui at that time"; Florencio IDOATE, *La brujería en Navarra...*, *op. cit.*, p. 48. The documents are in a very poor state of preservation, and I have not been able to confirm the reference given by Paul Arzak.

that comprise the process, one can find the variants *"aquer larre"*, *"aquerrlarre"*, *"aquerlarre"*, *"aquel larre"*, *"aquelarre"*, *"aquerlarrea"* and *"aquerlarria"*,[144] as well as expressions such as "going to the field of *aquer larre*"[145] or "going to the meeting [*junta*] and field they call *aquerlarrea*", the latter being included in the sentence against Martin de Barazarte.[146]

In the seventeenth century, after the Zugarramurdi trials, the word *"aquelarre"* or *"akelarre"* became the most common name for witches' meetings both in Spanish and Basque, but that is another story, or history. In fact, it is one that still needs to be properly researched taking into account the sources presented here; the works by Azurmendi, Henningsen and Paul—which treat the word as an "invention" ignoring De Lancre's, Landemont's and Farreny's previous publications—now appear even more clearly insufficient.[147]

Returning to the thread of the discussion, it is striking that the "field of *aquer larre*" and the female figure co-presiding over the meetings in that field feature together in the testimony of Maria Miguel de Orexa just as the *Lane de Boc* and the "Deviless" do in the summary of Estebene de Cambrue's statement. Although it should be borne in mind that Maria Miguel did not mention the "field of *aquer larre*" until the last part of her interrogation, which lasted at least two days, and that the records of her statement were translated from Basque, one could venture that both the inhabitants of Intza and those of Amou, or at least some families of those small communities, could have preserved in their narratives and

---

[144] AGN, Tribunales Reales, Procesos, no. 071319, ff. 5r and 5v; 9r and 11r; 15v and 17r; 5v and 11v; 26r; 38v and 49r; 25r and 28v. It should be noted that the variants with the final "a" (the singular definite article in Basque) appear in the transcriptions that in principle preserve the translations of the statements made by the defendants in Pamplona before a different notary than the one they had in the palace of Andueza.

[145] *Ibid.*, 5v.

[146] «[...] *ir a la junta y campo que llaman aquerlarrea*»; *ibid.*, 209r.

[147] Mikel AZURMENDI, *Nombrar, embrujar. Para una historia del sometimiento de la cultura oral en el País Vasco*, Irún, Alberdania, 1993, pp. 220 ff.; Mikel AZURMENDI, «La invención de la brujería como akelarre», *Bitarte. Revista cuatrimestral de humanidades*, no. 4, 1995, pp. 15–37; Gustav HENNINGSEN, «El invento de la palabra *aquelarre*», RIEV, no. 9, 2012, pp. 54–65; Juainas PAUL, «El aquelarre, una invención afortunada», *op. cit.*

beliefs about witches elements of a stage prior to the diabolisation of the latter.

Indeed, we have just seen that Maria Miguel de Orexa confessed that:

> When she was about ten years old, Maria de Chiqui Balda, grandmother of this deponent, being at the time of her death, called her and told her that this declarant should take charge of the office of witch that she had done in her time, [...] that *she had to take charge of the said office because otherwise her soul could not be torn out of her*.[148]

This last statement escapes from the stereotype, from the usual script of the declarations collected in contemporary trials. However, we find a similar deposition in an Italian trial from 1390. Two women, Sibillia and Pierina, were tried in Milan on two occasions, in 1384 and 1390.[149] They declared that "every week, on the night between Thursday and Friday", they went with "Oriente and her hateful company". They called these meetings *"ludus"* ('game') and Oriente *"domina ludi"* ('lady of the game'), to whom they made reverence "bowing their heads" and saying: "Be well, Madonna Oriente"; to which Oriente replied: "You are welcome, my daughters".[150]

Besides confessing that "the Lady teaches the members of the company the powers of herbs", shows them "all the things they ask her about illnesses, thefts and *maleficia*" and "predicts future things", Pierina stated that "living and dead men [...] attended the game", as well as "animals of all species, except asses and foxes". On this subject, Sibillia declared:

> To the same company came also, two by two, animals of every species except the asses, for these bore the cross, and that if even one of them were missing, the whole world would be destroyed.

---

[148] See n. 126 above.

[149] The original Latin document on the trials against Sibillia and Pierina remains unpublished. For the following lines, I have used the abridged Italian translation published in Luisa MURARO, *La Signora del gioco. La caccia alle streghe interpretata dalle sue vittime*, Milan, La Tartaruga, 2006, pp. 200–206.

[150] The words in Latin are recorded in Marina MONTESANO, *Classical Culture and Witchcraft in Medieval and Renaissance Italy*, London-New York, Palgrave Macmillan (Palgrave Historical Studies in Witchcraft and Magic), 2018, p. 190. For a similar case from the fifteenth century, see Carlo GINZBURG, *Historia nocturna. Un desciframiento del aquelarre*, Barcelona, Muchnik Editores, 1991, part 2, I, pp. 88–89.

Perhaps in relation to such a *quorum*, in 1390 Pierina also confessed that:

> She had started going to the game around the age of sixteen, when *her aunt Agnesina sent her in her place, otherwise not being able to die.*

16 An Unknown Lacuna

Ludwig Wittgenstein wrote around 1933: "The difficulty in philosophy is to say no more than we know".[151]

After this brief but exhaustive journey through the fifteenth and sixteenth-century sources on the *Lane de Boc*, the time has come to return to the trial of Pes de Guoythie and Condesse de Beheythie. In the latter's statement, we read that "she had been to *boque lane* fully three times".[152] Unfortunately, the document provides little more detail on this subject. Condesse said that "they [plural] used to go to *boque lane* on Sundays". Thus we know that, in principle, it was a collective activity or gathering on specific days; but who attended? All kinds of people, only sorcerers or only women? It can be deduced that the interrogators knew the meaning of her testimony, for they did not ask any further questions about it.

We are also told that "going to *boquelane*" was a "sin", no more and no less. That is, it does not seem to be a trivial matter, since it was necessary to "confess" having done it, but neither does it seem to be of any great significance in the proceedings against Condesse; the main crime, the one that justified the exception to the law and her condemnation to undergo the hot iron ordeal, was murder by magical or sorcerous means. This contrasts with the trials of the fifteenth century, where the meetings and the denial of the faith that took place in them were the determining elements in many of the cases.

On the other hand, we read that Condesse "acknowledged by God and by her soul that she had never confessed that sin to us *because she had no power to confess it*". Pierina, whose case we have just discussed, appears to have made a similar claim in 1390. According to the sentence of her trial, in addition to going out with the "company" of "the Lady", the woman

---

[151] Ludwig WITTGENSTEIN, *The Blue and the Brown Books*, Oxford, Basil Blackwell, 1967, p. 45.

[152] See n. 57 above.

declared that she had made a pact with a demon, but said that "she had never confessed that fact *because she had no power to do so in any way*".[153]

Yet, neither in Condesse's declaration, nor anywhere else in the 1370 appeal letter, is there any mention of a devil, divinity, monster, ghost or spirit, with the exception of the "*boq(ue)*" which is part of the term "*boquelane*". Of course, the sources presented in this discussion lead us to imagine multiple hypotheses; however, for the time being, we have no way of knowing the specific traits of the beliefs referred to in Condesse's statements, nor the state, form or degree of prevalence they had in 1370 in the land of Mixe.

Nevertheless, the most remarkable characteristic of this process might be that we already know of all the features it presents—confessions under torture; judges who know or are ready to believe the narratives told by the defendants; metamorphosis into animals; child-killing; poisoning; collectively performed *maleficia*; use of ointments; toads; herbs; external coercion; the buck goat; and the attendance at meetings on specific days and in specific places—but we have never before encountered all these elements together in such an early source. Furthermore, we will have to wait more than fifty years to find them together again, in the 1420s, at the time when current historiography places the beginnings of the great European witch-hunts.

In fact, those features appear more or less simultaneously in sources from three different places: in Catalonia (in 1424), in the legal statutes from the Vall d'Àneu; in Italy (in 1428), in the trial held in Todi against Matteuccia di Francesco; and in the Alpine valleys in Switzerland, in Hans Fründ's chronicle of the witch-hunts from the 1420s.

In this last source, Hans Fründ—writing in the early 1430s—describes the persecution of witches in the Valais including, among other things, child-killings; use of ointments; *maleficia*; metamorphosis into wolves; collective meetings, and pacts with the Devil where the "evil spirit" appeared to the witches "in the shape of a black animal, sometimes in the form of a bear, sometimes in the form of a *wider* [buck sheep]".[154]

---

[153] Luisa MURARO, *La Signora del gioco...*, *op. cit.*, p. 205.

[154] «*Und ist inen der boess geist den merteil erschinnen in eines swartzen tieres wise, etwenn in forme eines beren, etwenn in forme eines widers*»; Martine OSTORERO et al. (eds.), *L'imaginaire du sabbat...*, *op. cit.*, pp. 30–45.

In the Italian case, in the records of the trial against Matteuccia di Francesco (1428), we read that she was accused of child-killing, metamorphosing into a fly through the application of an ointment and going to the walnut tree at Benevento by riding on a demon in the shape of a buck goat. In Benevento, "she meets lots of *stregas* [witches] and enchanted spirits and infernal demons and *Luciferum maiorem*, who, presiding, orders Matteuccia and others to go around killing infants and doing other evil things".[155]

Lastly, in Catalonia we find the already partially mentioned legal statutes of the Vall d'Àneu (1424):

> Of all these crimes there is evidence from the trials and confessions of the defendants; [...]. Firstly we establish and order, if from now on it is found that a man or woman of the said valley goes with the *bruxes* [witches] by night to the *boch de Biterna* and pays homage to him, taking him as lord, disowning the name of God, and the same if he gives apples to [*pomarà*] or kills small children by night or by day, [...] and the same if he gives *metzines* [medicines, poisons], that such man or woman who commits such crimes shall lose his body, [...] be put to the fire and his body turned to dust.[156]

Oscar Wilde made one of his characters affirm that "truth is rarely pure and never simple", and that if this were not so, modern literature would be "a complete impossibility". No doubt lacunae or gaps are, along with

---

[155] «[...] *et ibi invenit quam plurimas stregas et ipsos incantatos ac demones infernales et Luciferum maiorem, qui presidendo precipit ipsi [Matteuccia] et aliis ut vadant circumquamque ad infants destruendos et alia mala facienda*»; Domenico MAMMOLI, *Processo alla strega Matteuccia di Francesco (Todi, 20 marzo 1428)*, Spoleto, Fondazione Centro italiano di studi sull'alto medioevo, 2013, pp. 26–29.

[156] «[...] *de tots aquests crims se apar per procesos confesio[ns] pròpries dels dellats; [...].Primerament stablim e ordonam si d'aquí avant serà atrobat que hom o fembra de la dita vall vaga ab les bruxes de nit al boch de Biterna e aquel farà homenatge, prenent-lo per senyor, renegant lo nom de Déu, e noresmeyns que pomarà o matarà inffants petits de nit o de dia, e darà gatirnons o buxols, e aixi mateyx darà metzines, que tal hom o fembra qui semblants delictes cometrà perda lo cors, [...] sia mes al foch e del seu cors feta polvera*»; Pau CASTELL, «*Sortílegas, divinatrices...*», *op. cit.*, p. 238; English translation in Pau CASTELL, « "Wine vat witches...», *op. cit.*, pp. 176–177; the translation has been modified where necessary.

contingency, the most interesting part of History, if not History itself. Nevertheless, perhaps for this very reason, the satisfaction of believing that one has filled a lacuna by following certain traces is not comparable to the pleasure of discovering one, hitherto unknown, and admiring it... brutal, violent, imposing.

AGN, Comptos, Documentos, caj. 87, no. 62, 2, f. 1r.

AGN, Comptos, Documentos, caj. 87, no. 62, 2, f. 2r.

AGN, Comptos, Documentos, caj. 87, no. 62, 2, f. 3r.

AGN, Comptos, Documentos, caj. 87, no. 62, 2, f. 4r.

AGN, Comptos, Documentos, caj. 87, no. 62, 2[157]

f. 1r [...]/ [...] de las [...] / [...] dixo las palaures qui seguy au seynnor [...] / «[...] Willem Arnaut, filli d'Ilharrart d'Ilharre es estat acusat de la mort de Pey- / [ronne d]aune d'Ilharrart, sa nebode. La quoau acusacion lo dit Willem Arnaut a confessat la dite mort / [...] luys no degudementz et ben cas de traytion, segunt que plus plenerementz es contengut / [...] cartes deu confes, dit e autreyat per la boque lo dit Willem [Arnaut e]n presentes de uos e de la bone Cort / de Micxe. Per lo quoau confes lo dit Willem Arnaut es sentenciat per la b[one Cort de] Micxe que sie arrastrat entro / au pe de la forque et a qui sie penut segunt au cas aparthiey [...] autreyat de sa boque / en Cort plenere aparthiey. E cum lo dit Willem Arnaut, beden que here sentenciat a mort segunt dit hes, a / descarguament de sa anime e per amor que Diu lo pay lo uuylle perdonar sous pecatz e sous fay- / lhimientz, en Cort plenere ayhe confessat e autreyat e dit de sa boque chetz nuylle destrece / que lo seynnor no ho danhe, que et dit Willem Arnaut here faytiler e sabe far faytilhes e que l'aben / mustrat a ffar faytiles Pes de Guoythie e Condesse, daune de Beheytie, parropians d'Illharre, / speciaumentz que en lo mes de may qui a [...] passa que et dit Willem Arnaut e lo dit Pes e Condese / heren anatz [...]qui aben escanat l'enfant / de Guixon d'Eli[çague e de Domenge, sa moylher, segunt que plus] plenerementz es conte- / [ngut] [...]at en sa darrer / [...]me, la tenor [de la quoau] carte [de mot a mot es en la maner]e que segt: "Conegude / [cause sie a totz que] en presence de mi, notari, e deus t]estimonis deius escriutz dentz lo castet de Garris, / [Guillem Arnaut, filli] d'Ilharrart dixo las palaures qui seguen a l'ondrat e saui Bernat Santz de Lacxague, / baylle de Micxe per lo mot redoptable seynnor monsseynnor de Labrit, bescopte de Thartas: 'Seynnor / en baylle, aysi es la cause que hen lo mes de may qui passat es sim bincou a mi Pes de Guoy- / thie e Condesse, daune de Beheythie, parropiantz d'Ilharre, e dixonme que anassem es- / canar l'enfant de Guixon d'Elicague e de Domenge, sa moylher, los quoaus desus nomiatz / e lo predit qui parle anem la medixe noeyt e quant son en la porte bantz, dize la dite Con- / desse que demorassem en la dite porte e que here hentrare e, si no pode here deliurar, que etz en- / trassen. Apres aco, dit que ba hentrar la dite Condesse per debut lo sola de l'ostau en forme / de can et hun paucg estat la dite Condesse baixir e baus dize que escanat l'abe lo dit / enfant'. Lo quoau soberdit baylle domana au dit Willem Arnaut si dize per malebolence, dixo a Diu / e a sa anime que no, saubant

---

[157] Transcription by Roberto Ciganda; for ease of reading, abbreviations have been developed and punctuation marks and capital letters added.

que no bole este carcat dequet pecat, car bole mes que etz portassen / la lor penitence que no et. E de totes e sengles las causes desus dites, lo dit baylle requeri mi, / notari, qu'en ne fes public esturment. Ço fo feyt dentz lo castet de Garris, XII dies en lo mes de / julli, anno Domini Mº CCCº LXXº. Testimonis son de ço: Willem Arnaut d'Array e Gaussernaut de Guabat, be- / zinis de Guarris, e jo, Bernasantz d'Urruthie, notari public per l'auctoritat reyau de las terres / de Nauarre de ça portz, qui aqueste carte escriscuy, etc." E cum bos seynnor en baylle, thincatz / en bostre poder los diitz Pes de Guoythie e Condesse, daune de Beheythie, los quoaus son faytilers / e vsen de grat mestir e an feytz motz dampnatges de diuerses maneyres e conditions. E / me dix los ditz Pes e Condesse en presence de bos et de notari jurat et de bons testimonis[158] */ f. 2r axhen autrerat esser bertat co que lo sobrediit Willem Arnaut a confessat; e de mes axhen dit e con- / fessat de los propris boques aber feyt d'autres mortz e faytiles e mes diuers dampnatges, se- / gunt plus plenementz es contengut en cartes publiques feytes per man de notari jurat, la / tenor de la primere carte es en la manere seguent: "Notum sit contis quod anno Domini Mº CCCº LXX,º XX et III*[es] */ dies en lo mes de julli, dentz lo castet de Guarris, en presence de mi, notari, e deus testimonis deius escriutz, l'on- / drat e saui Monaut, sire de Naquole, loc thient de baylle de Micxe per l'ondrat e saui Bernat Santz de / Lacxague, baylle de Micxe per lo mot redoptable seynnor monsseynnor de Labrit, etc., dixo las palaures / qui seguen a Pes, filli de l'ostau de Guoythie d'Ilharre: 'Pes, jo ey audit a Willem Arnaut, filli d'Ilha- / rrart, e a confessat a sa dardere fin, en presence de bons gentz au pe de la forque, que tu es fay- / tiler e huses de faytiles e as escanatz enfantz am luys e am d'autres persones per que si parasces / tues a tan que tu mag boylles dizer e mustrar aquetz qui saps que tan sien asi que / la toe anime sie descarcade'. Lo quoau Pes de Guoythie dixo e hespono au sobredit locg thi- / ent de baylle estan en la cambre segut sober lo heyt lo dit Pes qui parle sieys nuylle des- / trece que lo seynnor ni houtre per loys no ho danhe, etc. Lo sobredit Pes qui parle dixo que bey pode / abe VII o hoeyt antz que encontre Condesse daune d'Aguerre d'Ilharrart en vne carrere es- / trete fazen las faytiles heuba dize la dite Condesse que puys a qui here escadut bertadere- / mentz cumbie que aprencos de far faytiles o, si no bole far, que et morire o que bador meset, lo / quoau Pes de Guoythie espono que mes bole aprener domestir. Item apres dixo que et fo au loc / quent het lo dit Pes*

---

[158] Manuscript on the back (testimony of proceedings in the Tribunal de la Cort in 1376), very lost: «*Anno Domini Mº CCCº LXXº VIº, XXº dia de jenero, en Pomplona, en Cort [...] beydo este processo, la dicha [...] fecha pora en la [...] de Sant Anton [...] de dios conssegrados [...] en [...] juyzio [...] d'Aramburu*».

qui parle e Willem Arnaut, filli d'Ilharrart, e Condese daune de Beheytie / d'Ilharre escanan l'enfant de Domenge d'Eliçague, de la parropie d'Ilharre. Item apres dixo / a Diu e a sa anime lo predit qui parle que et e Pejenauton, seynnor d'Aphatie d'Ilharre, escanan / l'enfant d'Ihirçe de Camou. Item apres dixo a Diu e a sa anime que et qui parle e Perar de Hui- / guoe et Condesse daune de Beheytie d'Ilharre escanan vn enfant a Biscay Hiriart. Item / apres dixo lo predit qui parle que Hilharre e a Biscay et a Sarricoete que et qui parle e Willem Arnalt, filli / d'Ilharrart, e Condesse daune de Beheytie e Per Arnaut, seynnor d'Aphatie d'Ilharre, an torude la pome / d'onguan. Item lo soberdit locg thient de baylle lo domana sin sabe plus, dixo que no car / taber dixcx cum dequetz e no dize per nuylle malbolence quius por tanhe sauban per descarguar la / soe anime. E de totes e sengles las causes desus dites, lo soberdit locg thient de baylle reque- / ri mi notari queu ne fes public esturment. Ço fo ffeyt l'an, die e locg sobredit. Testimonis son de / ço: maestre Johan de Sormendi, Guaseruant de Guabat, seynnor juen d'Etchesarri, Willem Pe de Casemayor, / Santz Lop de Miramont, beziis de Guarr[is], e jo, Bernat Santz d'Urruthie, notari public per l'autoritat / reyau de las terres de Nauarre de ca portz, qui aqueste carte escriscuy, etc." La tenor de la seguente / carte es en la manerie seguent: "Notum sit cuntis quod anno Domini M^o CCC^o LXX^a, XX et IIIes dies en lo / mes de julli, dentz lo castet de Guarris, en presence de mi, notari, e deus testimonis deius escriutz / l'ondrat e saui Monaut, seynnor de Naquole, locg thient de baylle de Micxe per l'ondrat e saui Bernat / Santz de Lacxague, baylle de Micxe per lo mot redoptable seynnor monsseynnor de Labrit, etc., dixo / las palaures qui seguen a Condesse daune de Beheytie d'Ilharre: 'Condesse, jo ey audit a / Willem Arnaut, filli d'Ilharrart, defunt, e a confessat au pe de la forque a sa dardere fin / en presence de bones gentz que tu es faytilere e huses de faytiles e as escanatz enfantz / am loys e am d'autres persones per que si parasce tues a tan que tu mag boylles dizer e mustrar / aquetz qui saps que tan sien asii que la toe anime sie descarcade dequet pecat'. La quoau Con- / desse dixo et hespono au soberdit locg thient de baylle, estan en la cambre do seynor / sieys nuylle destrece alox que lo seynnor ni houtre per luys no ho danhe quent parlanhe, la sober- / dite Condesse dixo que here fo au locg am Pes de Guoythie e am Willem Arnaut filli d'Ilharrart / quent escanan l'enfant de Domenge d'Elicague d'Ilharre. Item apres dixo la predite qui / f. 3r *qui parle que Willem Arnaut sire d'Etchaluçuui de la parropie de Guabat es faytiler e vse de / faytiles. Item dixo per medixs departhit que Per Arnaut seynnor de Hinguoe here tambey fay- / tiler e usauhe de faytiles. Item dixo per medix departhit la predite qui parle que Per Arnaut seyhnor / d'Aphatie* *d'Ilharre here faytiler e usauhe de faytiles. Item apres dixo la predite qui parle / que here e Pethrii Guoythiie e Willem Arnaut filli d'Ilharrart e Per Arnaut seynnor d'Apathie de la / parropie d'Ilharre e Per Arnaut sire de Hinguoe e Willem Arnaut sire d'Etchaluçuui de Guabat aben torude la pome d'onguan, co es assaber Hilharre e a Guabat. Item apres dixo la predite qui parle / que here prenco per Carbeda qui passat hes, dus crepautz heus, la cose e quent sen cuytz / quen bagua la carn; e dequet bro fazen las faytiles; e quent se bolen far autes semblan- / ces etz, se laben dequet bro las mas e los julhs e, alox hetz, se fen semblantz de cas e de / guatz. Item apres dixo que here heree estade a boque lane bey tres betz. Item apres dixo a / Diu e a sa anime que nustemps aquet pecat nos confesse car no abe poder de confesa. Item / dize que solen anar a boquelane lo dimenx. Item apres dixo que no sabe plus car sin sabes ca bey / dixo et cum deus nomiatz desus, interroguades si dixo per malebolence quius portauhe ni / per aute cas, dixo que no sauban per descarcar sa anime. E de totz e sengles las causes desus dites / lo sober dit locg thient de baylle requeri mi notarii quen ne fes public esturment. Co ffo ffeyt / l'an, die e locg soberdit. Testimonis son de co: Santz Lop de Mira- mont, Arnaut Cabant, bezinis / de Guarris, e jo Bernat d'Urruthie, notarii public per l'autoritat reyau de las terres de Nauarre deça / portz qui aqueste carte escriscuy etc." Per la quoau cause bos pregui humiumentz eps requeri per lo segra- / ment qui feyt abetz, que uos deus ditz Pes de Guoythie e de Condesse daune de Beheytie / bayllatz far justizie de los cas a tau cum aus cas que etz an feytz e autreyatz aperthiey; car / dic que puys que lo dit Willem Arnaut en lo cas de la mort a confessat e mostrat que etz son faytiles, et / ansi etz medix de los boques an aquero am d'autres males obres que an feyt, autreyat e confesatt, / dic que schetz nuylle autre dilation ades ce serementz los deuetz far sentenciar a bostre Cort e far / justizie de los cos tau cum du cas aperthiey, car dic que far acy debetz per nostre dreyturie; e / nuylle a razon que etz digue ni perpausien en contre las causes desus dites a lor no deu hagu- / dar ni baler ni a mi perjudicar ni nozer, abantz ce sermentz debetz far justizie de los cos tant per / co que lo dit Willem Arnaut en sa dardere fin a dit e demostrat, tant per la confession de los boques e per los / malificis que etz an feyt entro a cii e poyren far de cii en abant; e dic que far ar debetz, e de ço re- / queri judicii de nostre cort». Item aqui medix en la dite cort Monaut de Picassany di- / zen e parlan en nom et hen birtz deu sober dit Pes de Guoythie e de Condesse daune de / Beheythie de la parropie d'Ilharre, dixo las palaures qui seguen: «Seynnor en baylle, sau- / bi e protesti tot mon dret e de ma parthide e no departeu de ma protestation, bos cum a seynnor thin- / cossetz an astatz en uostre poder Pes de Guoythie e Condesse daune de Beheythie de la parro- / pie d'Ilharre sieys ningun quereylant ni clamant, per la quoau cause acuse lo dit procurador deu / seynnor en dizen que son faytiles e faytileres. Los quoaus dizen a la soe acusation hon ja diu / no don que sien taus e plus cum los ayhe acusat e mustratz Willem Arnaut filli d'Ilharrart par fay- / tiles e faytileres. E lo dit procurador los acuse par le son dit chetz nuylli autre quereylant ni clamant / dic que nuylle acusation ni mustration que lo dit Willem Arnaut ayhe feyt aus ditz arrastatz ni / lo procurador alleguie ni mustrie dic que no a locg; e per aqueste arrazon que cum et sic estat mur- / trer desisanc estan tutor e ministrador de Peyronne daune d'Iharrart et ayhe feyt / la dite mort per amor que a bos los beys de la dite Peyronne, sa nebode; e cum et ayhe feyt / tau cas e per lo cas sie sentenciat e judiat a mort per traydor en la cort de Micxe, dic que tolu a- / cusation feyte per lo dit Willem Arnaut aus ditz arrastatz, dic que no deu aber locg tau testimo- / f. 4r niatge de nuyll traydor qui face tau mustration ni acusation abantz es nullc e de / nulle balor, car tan es lo for e la costum, que nuylli traydor no deu esse audit ni son testi- / moinatge no deu baler; e si a faze, dic que es nullc e de nulle balor. E cum lo dit Willem / Arnaut los portauhe malebolence au dit Pes e Condesse per co que heren sabençes de la mort / feyte, au quoau bolen metre a mort. E plus alleguan e dizen pusque no hi a autre clamant / ni autre quereylant, mos deuhetz dar per soutz e per quitis e condampnar me lo procurador de / las messions de la balor de L libres de LX negres o tant cum jo auseri aber a. Item a co que diitz / que etz an cofessat de lor boque e an dit, dic que tau dit no a locg sauban la loi au nor car co que / an diit, si dit an, an dit per force e per destrece que lo seynnor los a dat segunt dixen, lo quoau / par en los menbres que son romputz e nafratz en los cos fortementz per que dic que tau dit ap[res] / que abosse dit, no a locg abantz es nulle e de nulle balor etant per lo for etant per costume e per / bone arazon. E a co que ditz que cum a franque persone a dit, jo dic que no car abantz estauhe en la pre- / son et hestan en la preson, nuylli a res que dixos no deu aber locg; ne nuylle obligation que fes, / ne nuylle acusation que lo procurador face ni lo seynnor, dic que no deu aber locg; e si a fey, es di- / z en deu esser quitis puys autre clamant ni arrancurant no an. E plus quent son en- / queritz en cort pleynne per lo seynnor per cada arthicle que dit auen, dixon de no e denegan / en presence deu seynnor e de la cort, car a loy heren chetz temo e chetz dopte e fore de / preson. Item dic plus que puys no an autre quereylant ni no son prauhatz ni atentz en lo dit / cas mos deuhetz dar per soutz e per quitis, totes betz cumdampnan a las mesios qui a dat au / cas aparthiey audit procurador, las quoaus estimii L libres de LX negres o tant cum jo auseri / aber a; e si lo dit procurador ni lo dit acusador bo* dize que bos no mos deyatz dar per quitis, / jo dic que sii e requeri judicii de vostre cort». Et en clauses las dites parthides en las dites / arrazons, la mayor parthide de la Cort de Micxe deu per judicii tant per la confession dite per Willem Arnaut / filli d'Ilharrart, feyte a sa fin, que lo dit Willem Arnaut e Pes filli de Guoythie e Condesse, daune de Behey- / tie, aben mort l'enfant de Guixon d'Eliçague e de Domenge, sa moylher, et heren faytiles e faytileres, / que lo dit Pes e Condesse bayhen a Hurcoyn do die de la date de queste carte en vn mes et / aqui leuien lo fer caut; que ay, si etz no son tortures ni merentz de la dite mort deu dit filli / de Guixon de Eliçague, acusatz e confessatz per lo dit Willem Arnalt, filli d'Ilharrart, ni etz no son fayti- / les, ni nustemps no an vsat de faytiles far, abantz son bo[n]s e leyaus; e si parasce son per taus / prauhatz bons, que sien quitis; en lo cas que no sien prauhatz per bons ni per leyaus, que lo seynnor / ne faze justizie de los cos segunt au cas aparthiey. E si no fos per l'acusation de la dite mort / per arrazon de las faytilles, darem per sentencie que fes discossen segunt los for e la costume de la / terre de Micxe segunt au cas aparthie, a mossen Sent Johan de Sordoe o a mossen Sent Johan de / Surçaytoquie. La menor parthide de la cort deu per judici que puys autre acusador no han / sauban lo procurador deu seynnor, que nuylhe acusation deu seynnor no deu perjudicar a / son subgit si no que abos autre acusador e si a faze dicem que es dicen lor man e lor boque / a mossen Sent Johan de Sordoe o a mossen Sent Johan de Surçaytoquie, lo dam per quitis. E lo dit pro- / curador thiense per agreuiat deus judiciis e sentencies de la mayor parthide e de la meno[r] au / ca e apara de la nostre cort de Micxe a la bostre bone cort de Nauarre per que suplicam a la vostre nob- / le seynnorie que uos a cada hune de las parthides detz per sentencie co que a bos sera de bey bist de dret / e d'a razon; e asignam las dites parthides que a X dies apres la date de queste carte sien per / d'abant bos e porte la presente medix lo procurador, Marthin Gil d'Ureta, Miguel Guarcea de Burutay[n], / Willem Arnaut de Bassaguaytz e cada hun de lor no constrestan la present dos huns aus autres. E secg / la peu per lo dit Pes e Condesse medix Monaut de Picassaun, Marthin Guilh d'Ureta, Miguelh / Guarcea de Buruthayn, Willem Arnaut de Bassaguaytz, Arnaut Santz sire de Cahesauri e cada hun de lor no / contrastan la present, dos huns aus autres. Co ffo ffeyt a Garris, XX et IIII^{ta} dies en lo mes d'Ahost / anno Domini M° CCC° LXX°.[159]

---

[159] Manuscript on the back: «Au mot noble et poderos seynnor mosen Marthin d'Arthede, cabaler, guobernador de Nauarr. / Apeu de la Cort de Micx a la bone Cort de Nauarr».

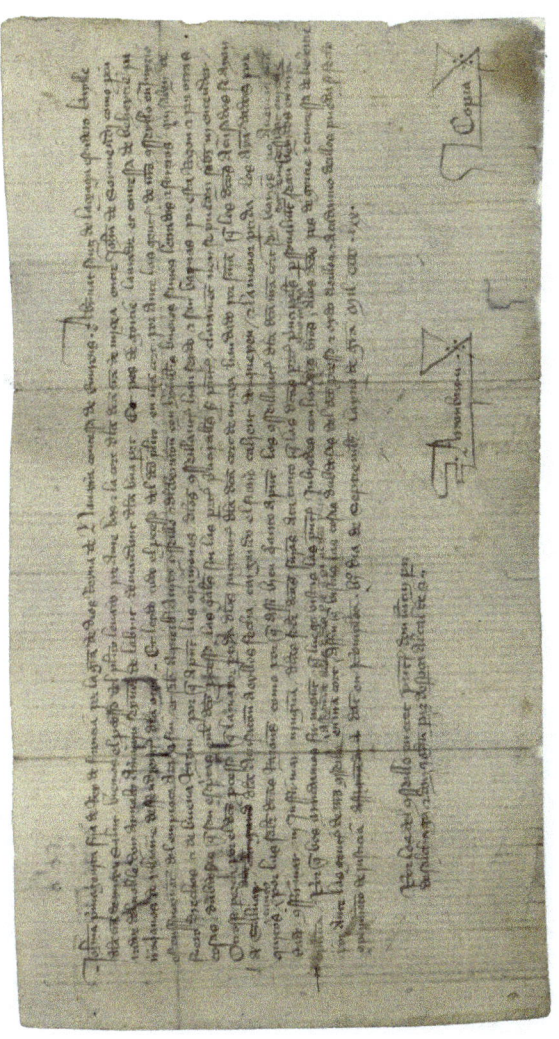

AGN, Comptos, Documentos, caj. 87, no. 62, 1

f. 1r Johanna, primogenita fija de Rey de Francia, por la gracia de Dios Reyna de Nauarra. Contessa de Euureus. A Bernat Santz de Lacxaga, escudero, baylle / de la terra de Micxa, salut. Viemos el processo del pleito leuado por ante vos a la cort de la dicha terra de Micxa entre Johan de Sormendi, como procu- / rador del noble don Arnalt Amaniu, seynnor de Labrit, demandant, de la una part, et Pes de Goitie. laurador, et Contessa de Beheytie, pa- / rroquianos de Ylharre, deffendientes, de la otra. Et leydo todo el processo del dicho pleito en nuestra cort por ante las gentes de nuestro consseyllo en juyzio / estenssiuament del empieço ata la fin et sober aqueill auido consseyllo et deliberation con hombres buenos, sauios, letrados et foreros qui saben de / fuero, drechos et de buena razon, porque a present las opiniones de los consseillantes han seydo et son barias, por esta razon et por otras / cosas dubdosas que son escriptas en el dicho proceso, los quoales, sin las partes principalles ser presentes, clarament non se pueden saber ni entender. / Otrossi parezca por el dicho processo que la mayor partida de los jugantes de la dicha cort de Micxa han dado por sentencia que los dichos acusados se ayan / de saluar [de la a cargand (crossed out)] de la acusacion a eyllos fecha cargando el fierro calient d'Orqueyen et la menor partida los ayan dados por / quitos, tanto por las sobre dichas razones como porque assi bien quoanto a present los consseillantes de la dicha nuestra cort son barios, no auemos man- / dado confirmar ni inffirmar ninguna de las sobre dichas sentencias, ata tanto que las dichas partes principales perssonalment, segunt de nescessidat conuiene, sean venidos en nuestra / presencia. Por que vos mandamos firmement que, luego vistas las presentes, inbiedes con hombres vuestros a cierto dia a los dichos Pes de Goitie et Contessa de Beheitie / por ante las gentes de nuestro consseillo en nuestra cort, assignando a las dichas partes que para al dicho parezcan affin que, vistas las cosas dubdosas del dicho processo et oydo a eillos et a cadauno deillos, pueda ser fecho / complimiento de justicia. [Assignado a (crossed out)]. Dat. en Pamplona. VIº dia de septiembre, l'ayno de gracia Mil CCC LXX.

Por los del consseillo en cort presentes: don Martin Periz / de Solchaga et don Johan Periz d'Esparça, alcaldes.

Aramburu [signature]. *Copia.*

Bibliography

Peter AINSWORTH and Godfried CROENEN (eds.), *The Online Froissart*, version 1.5, Sheffield, HRIOnline, 2013, http://www.hrionline.ac.uk/online froissart.
Eudaldo ARANDA, «La quema de brujas de 1507. Notas en torno a un enigma histórico», *Huarte de San Juan*, no. 17, 2010, pp. 411–422.
Darío de AREITIO, «Las brujas de Ceberio», *Revista internacional de los estudios vascos* (RIEV), vol. 18, no. 4, pp. 654–664.
Dan ATTRELL and David PORRECA (eds.), *Picatrix. A Medieval Treatise on Astral Magic*, Pennsylvania, The Pennsylvania State University Press, 2019.
Mikel AZURMENDI, *Nombrar, embrujar. Para una historia del sometimiento de la cultura oral en el País Vasco*, Irun, Alberdania, 1993.
Mikel AZURMENDI, «La invención de la brujería como akelarre», *Bitarte. Revista cuatrimestral de humanidades*, no. 4, 1995, pp. 15–37.
Marc BADAL, *Cuadernos de viaje. Fragmentos y pasajes históricos sobre semillas*, San Sebastian, Haziera, 2016.
Etienne BALUZE, *Capitularia Regum Francorum*, II, Paris, Pierre de Chiniac, 1677.
Luciano BANCHI (ed.), *Le prediche volgari di San Bernardino da Siena*, Siena, Tip. edit all'inseg. di S. Bernardino, 1888.
José Miguel de BARANDIARÁN, *Diccionario ilustrado de mitología vasca*, Bilbao, Editorial La Gran Enciclopedia Vasca, 1972.
José Miguel de BARANDIARÁN, *Brujería y brujas: Testimonios recogidos en el País Vasco*, San Sebastian, Txertoa, 1994.
Ander BERROJALBIZ, *Los herejes de Amboto. «Luteranos» en el año 1500*, Arre, Pamiela, 2016.

Ander BERROJALBIZ and Joseba SARRIONANDIA, *La hija de los herejes*, Arre, Pamiela, 2018.

François BORDES, *Sorciers et sorcieres: Procès de sorcellerie en Gascogne et Pays Basque*, Toulouse, Éditions Privat, 1999.

Robin BRIGGS, «"Many reasons why". Witchcraft and the problems of multiple explanation» in Jonathan BARRY, Marianne HESTER and Gareth ROBERTS (eds.), *Witchcraft in Early Modern Europe. Studies in Culture and Belief*, Cambridge, Cambridge University Press (Past and Present Publications), 1996, pp. 49–63.

Pau CASTELL, «*Sortilegas, divinatrices* et *fetilleres*: Les origines de la sorcellerie en Catalogne», *Cahiers de Recherches Médiévales et Humanistes*, no. 22, 2011, pp. 217–241.

Pau CASTELL, *Orígens i evolució de la cacera de bruixes a Catalunya (segles XV–XVI)*, doctoral thesis, Barcelona, Universitat de Barcelona, 2013.

Pau CASTELL, «"Wine vat witches suffocate children": The Mythical Components of the Iberian Witch», *eHumanista*, no. 26, 2014, pp. 170–195.

Roberto CIGANDA, «Introducción» in *Archivo General de Navarra. Sección de Comptos. Registro n.º 7 (1300)*, San Sebastian, Eusko Ikaskuntza (Fuentes Documentales Medievales del País Vasco, 129), 2006, pp. III–XLIII.

Adémar de CHABANNES, «Historia Francorum» (lib. III, cap. 59) in *Monumenta Germaniae Historica. Scriptores in folio* (MGH SS), vol. IV, Hannover, 1841, pp. 106–148.

Pierre de CHÂLONS, *Dictionnaire Breton-François du diocèse de Vannes*, Vannes, Jacques de Heuqueville, 1723.

Annie CHARNAY, «Criminalité et superstition à Gourdon-en-Quercy au début du XIVe siècle. L'histoire d'une sorcière» in *Mélanges historiques midi-pyrénéens*, Toulouse, Les Amis des Archives de la Haute-Garonne, 1992, pp. 79–93.

Annie CHARNAY, «Sept sorcières de Gourdon au début du XIVe siècle», *Bulletin de la Société des études du Lot*, CXV, 1994, pp. 17–49.

Amaury CHAUOU, «La religion souterraine à Saint-Malo en 1434», *Annales de Bretagne et des pays de l'Ouest*, CII, no. 2, 1995, pp. 107–112.

Ricardo CIERBIDE, «Introducción» in Arnaud d'OIHENART, *Notitia utriusque vasconiae*, Vitoria, Parlamento Vasco, 1992, pp. 15–99.

Ricardo CIERBIDE, «Fuentes histórico-documentales de la *Notitia utriusque vasconiae* y papeles inéditos de Arnaud d'Oihenart» in *Oihenarten laugarren mendeurrena. Cuarto centenario de Oihenart. Quatrième centenaire d'Oihénart*, Bilbao, Euskaltzaindia, 1994, pp. 575–612.

Norman COHN, *Europe's Inner Demons*, London, Pimlico, 1993.

John of DAMASCUS, «De strygibus» in Jacques Paul MIGNE, *Patrologia Graeca*, XCIV, cols. 1603–1604.

L. S. DAVIDSON and J. O. WARD (eds.), *The Sorcery Trial of Alice Kyteler*, Asheville, Pegasus Press, 2004.

André DU PRÉ, *Pouesies gascoues (1620)*, critical edition by Joan-Francés Courouau, Montpellier, Seccion Francesa de l'Associacion Internacionau d'Estudis Occitans, 1995.

Carmen ESPADA, *La vieja Narbona. De las sombras del alba, al resplandor de las hogueras*, Zaragoza, Certeza Libros, 1998.

EUSKALTZAINDIA (Real Academia de la Lengua Vasca), *Orotariko Euskal Hiztegia* (Diccionario General Vasco), www.euskaltzaindia.eus.

Maria Dolors FARRENY, *Processos de crims del segle XV a Lleida. Transcripció i estudi lingüístic*, Lleida, Institut d'Estudis Ilerdencs, 1986.

Pedro FERNÁNDEZ DE VILLEGAS, *La traducción del Dante de lengua toscana en verso castellano*, Burgos, Fadrique Alemán de Basilea, 1515.

Pierre-François FOURNIER, «Etymologie de sabbat, "réunion rituelle de sorciers"», *Bibliothèque de l'École des chartes*, CXXXIX, no. 2, 1981, pp. 247–249.

Jacques FRAYSSENGE, «Le sabbat des sorcières. La répression de l´hérésie à Millau au XVe siècle», *Heresis*, no. 44–45, pp. 189–206.

Carlos GARCÉS, *La mala semilla. Nuevos casos de brujas*, Barcelona, Tropo, 2013.

Ángel GARI, «Brujería en los Pirineos (siglos XIII al XVII). Aproximación a su historia», *Cuadernos de Etnología y Etnografía de Navarra*, no. 85, 2010, pp. 317–353.

Juan GARMENDIA, *Jentilak, sorginak eta beste*, San Sebastian, Elkar, 1994.

Jean de GARROS, *Pastourade gascoue sur la mort deu magnific é pouderous Anric quart deu nom rey de France é de Navarre*, Toulouse, Jean Boude, 1611.

Pey de GARROS, *Poesias gasconas*, Toulouse, Jammes Colomes, 1567.

Nicolas GERSHI, «Poisons, sorcières et lande de bouc», *Cahiers de recherches médiévales et humanistes*, no. 17, 2009, pp. 103–120.

Carlo GINZBURG, *Historia nocturna. Un desciframiento del aquelarre*, Barcelona, Muchnik Editores, 1991.

Carlo GINZBURG, *Los benandanti*, Guadalajara (Jalisco), Universidad de Guadalajara, 2005.

José GOÑI, «El tratado *De Superstitionibus* de Martín de Andosilla», *Cuadernos de etnología y etnografía de Navarra*, no. 9, 1971, pp. 249–322.

Eugène GOYHENECHE, «Un procès de sorcellerie à Ilharre en 1370», *Munibe*, XXIII, no. 4, 1971, pp. 457–461.

Joseph HANSEN, *Quellen und Untersuchungen zur Geschichte des Hexenwahns und der Hexenverfolgung im Mittelalter*, Bonn, Carl Georgi, 1901.

Ruth HARVEY and Linda PATERSON, *The Troubadour Tensos and Partimens: A Critical Edition*, Cambridge, D. S. Brewer, 2010.

Gustav HENNINGSEN, *El abogado de las brujas. Brujería vasca e inquisición española*, trad. de Marisa Rey-Henningsen, Madrid, Alianza Editorial, 2010.
Gustav HENNINGSEN, «El invento de la palabra *aquelarre*», RIEV, no. 9, 2012, pp. 54–65.
Ronald HUTTON, *The Witch. A History of Fear, from Ancient Times to the Present*, New Haven-London, Yale University Press, 2018.
Florencio IDOATE, *El señorío de Sarría*, Pamplona, Gráficas Iruña, 1959.
Florencio IDOATE, *Catálogo del Archivo General de Navarra. Sección de Comptos. Registros*, vol. LI (1258–1364) and vol. LII (1364–1535), Pamplona, Editorial Aramburu, 1974.
Florencio IDOATE, «Los brujos del Valle de Araiz» in *Brujología. Congreso de San Sebastián. Ponencias y comunicaciones*, Madrid, Seminarios y Ediciones S.A., 1975, pp. 53–68.
Florencio IDOATE, *La brujería en Navarra y sus documentos*, Pamplona, Institución Príncipe de Viana, 1978.
Florencio IDOATE, «Brujerías en la montaña de navarra en el siglo XVI», *Príncipe de Viana*, no. 223, 2001, pp. 299–321.
Pablo ILARREGUI and Segundo LAPUERTA (dirs.), *Fuero General de Navarra*, Pamplona, Imprenta Provincial, 1869.
Margaret H. KERR, Richard D. FORSYTH and Michael J. PLYLEY, «Cold Water and Hot Iron. Trial by Ordeal in England», *The Journal of Interdisciplinary History*, XXII, no. 4, 1992, pp. 573–595.
José María LACARRA, «Privilegio de Sancho el de Peñalen, confirmando al Santuario de San Miguel in Excelsis en la posesión de todos sus bienes. Lleva la confirmación de Sancho Ramírez. Año 1074», *Boletín de la comisión de monumentos históricos y artísticos de Navarra*, no. 1, 1927, pp. 558–563.
Pierre de LANCRE, *Tableau de l'inconstance des mauvais anges et demons*, Paris, Nicolas Buon, 1613.
L'abbé LANDEMONT (Pierre Larremendy), «Procès de sorcellerie en Basse-Navarre», *Revue de Béarn, Navarre et Lannes: partie historique de la Revue des Basses-Pyrénées et des Landes*, no. 1, 1883, pp. 49–54.
Ernest LANGLOIS (ed.), *Le roman de la rose*, Paris, Librairie Ancienne Édouard Champion, 1922.
Jean François LE GONIDEC, *Dictionnaire Français-Breton*, Saint-Brieuc, L. Prud'homme, 1847.
Peter T. LEESON, «Ordeals», *The Journal of Law and Economics*, vol. 55, no. 3, August 2012, pp. 691–714.
Guillaume de LORRIS and Jean de MEUN, *The Romance of the Rose*, trans. by Charles Dahlberg, Princeton, Princeton University Press, 1995.
Domenico MAMMOLI, *Processo alla strega Matteuccia di Francesco (Todi, 20 marzo 1428)*, Spoleto, Fondazione Centro italiano di studi sull'alto medioevo, 2013.

Walter MAP, *De nugis curialium*, London, Camdem Society, 1850.
Pierre de MARCA, *Histoire de Bearn*, Paris, Veuve Jean Camusat, 1640.
Franck MERCIER and Martine OSTORERO, *L'énigme de la Vauderie de Lyon. Enquête sur l'essor de la chasse aux sorcières entre France et Empire (1430–1480)*, Florence, Sismel-Edizioni del Galluzzo (Micrologus' Library), 2015.
Frédéric MISTRAL, *Lou Tresor dóu Felibrige*, Aix-en-Provence, Remondet-Aubin, 1886.
Marina MONTESANO, *Classical Culture and Witchcraft in Medieval and Renaissance Italy*, London-New York, Palgrave Macmillan (Palgrave Historical Studies in Witchcraft and Magic), 2018.
Luisa MURARO, *La Signora del gioco. La caccia alle streghe interpretata dalle sue vittime*, Milan, La Tartaruga, 2006.
Johannes NIDER, *Preceptorium divine legis*, Paris, André Bocard, 1531.
M.ª Isabel OSTOLAZA, *Colección Diplomática de Santa María de Rocesvalles (1127–1300)*, Pamplona, Institución Príncipe de Viana, 1978.
Martine OSTORERO, Agostino PARAVICINI and Kathrin UTZ TREMP (eds.), *L'imaginaire du sabbat. Edition critique des textes les plus anciens (1430 c.–1440 c.)*, Lausanne, Cahiers lausannois d'histoire médiévale, 1999.
Jonathan OTT, «Pharmañopo-Psychonautics: Human Intranasal, Sublingual, Intrarectal, Pulmonary and Oral Pharmacology of Bufotenine», *Journal of Psychoactive Drugs*, vol. 33, no. 3, July–September 2001 pp. 273–281.
Simin PALAY, *Dictionnaire du béarnais et du gascon modernes*, Pau, Imprimerie Marrimpouey Jeune, 1932.
Juan PAREDES, *Las narraciones de los* Livros de linhagens, Granada, Universidad de Granada, 1995.
Juainas PAUL, «El aquelarre, una invención afortunada», *Gerónimo de Uztariz*, no. 23–24, 2008, pp. 9–40.
Alexander PLUSKOWSKI, «Before the Werewolf Trials. Contextualising Shape-Changers and Animal Identities in Medieval North-Western Europe» in Willem de BLÉCOURT (ed.), *Werewolf Histories*, London-New York, Palgrave Macmillan (Palgrave Historical Studies in Witchcraft and Magic), 2015, pp. 82–118.
Regino of PRÜM, «De Ecclesiasticis Disciplinis» in Jacques Paul MIGNE, *Patrologia Latina*, CXXXII, cols. 185–404.
Tomás RIPOLL, *Bullarium ordinis ff. praedicatorum*, tomo III, Rome, Mainardi, 1731.
Martín de RIQUER, *Los trovadores. Historia literaria y textos*, Barcelona, Ariel, 2011.
Jeffrey B. RUSSELL, *Witchcraft in the Middle Ages*, Ithaca-London, Cornell University Press, 1988.
Julien SACAZE, *Inscriptions antiques des Pyrénées*, Toulouse, Imprimerie et Librairie Édouard Privat, 1892.

Fernando SÁNCHEZ, *Carlos II de Navarra. El rey que pudo dominar Europa*, Pamplona, Mintzoa, 2021.
José SARRIÓN, «Encantamientos, herbolarias y hechiceras en el Fuero de Cuenca y en los de su familia» in Javier ALVARADO (coord.), *Espacios y fueros en Castilla-La Mancha (siglos XI–XV). Una perspectiva metodológica*, Madrid, Ediciones Polifemo, 1995, pp. 387–404.
Félix SEGURA, «Hechicería y brujería en la Navarra medieval. De la superstición al castigo», RIEV, no. 9, 2012, pp. 284–304.
Snorri STURLUSON, *Heimskringla*, trans. by Alison Finley and Anthony Faulkes, London, Viking Socierty for Northern Research, University College London, 2011.
Filippo TAMBURINI, «Suppliche per casi di stregoneria diabolica nei registri della Penitenzieria e conflitti inquisitoriali», *Critica storica*, no. 23, 1986, pp. 605–659.
María TAUSIET, *Ponzoña en los ojos. Brujería y superstición en Aragón en el siglo XVI*, Zaragoza, Institución «Fernando el Católico», 2000.
Luis Manuel TEIXEIRA, «As pinturas dos tectos da igreja da Colegiada de Guimarães e a sua situação no contexto da pintura medieval peninsular» in *Congresso Histórico de Guimarães e a sua Colegiada. Actas. Volume IV. Comunicações*, Guimarães, 1981, pp. 449–467.
Jesús María USUNÁRIZ, «La caza de brujas en la Navarra moderna (siglos XVI–XVII)», RIEV, no. 9, 2012, pp. 306–350.
Oscar WILDE, *The Importance of Being Earnest*, London, Leonard Smithers & Co., 1899.
Ludwig WITTGENSTEIN, *The Blue and the Brown Books*, Oxford, Basil Blackwell, 1967.
Thomas WRIGHT (ed.), *A Contemporary Narrative of the Proceedings Against Dame Alice Kyteler, Prosecuted for Sorcery in 1324, by Richard de Ledrede, Bishop of Ossory*, London, The Camden Society, 1843.
Thomas WRIGHT and James O. HALLIWELL (eds.), *Reliquiae antiquae*, London, John Russell Smith, 1845.

Index

A
Abadie, Jeannette d', 15
Abalegui, 55
Abundance, Lady, 17, 19
accusatorial process, 29
AGN. *See* Archivo Real y General de Navarra (AGN)
Agramont, 3
Aguerre, Condesse d', 18, 66
Aherbelste (god), 34
Aizkorri, 47
akelarre. *See Aquer larre, Aquerlarre*
aker, akher, aquer. *See* buck goat, he-goat
Aker çaltua, 26, 47
Albi, Raymonde de S., 19
Albret, Arnaut Amanieu d' (Viscount of Tartas and Lord of Mixe), 9, 10, 13, 72
Alpine valleys, 59
Amezketa, 15
Amou, 45, 56
Anboto, 47
Andorra, 21, 38
Andueza, 47, 48, 56
Àneu, Vall d', 20, 36, 59, 60
Anotzibar, 50, 52
Apathie, Per Arnaut d', 19, 20, 22, 23, 68
apple (poisoned), 18, 20–23, 38, 60
Apuleius, 16
aquelarre. *See Aquer larre, Aquerlarre*
Aquer larre, Aquerlarre, 26, 27, 46, 54–56, 58
Aquerlurra, 26, 27
Aquitaine, Duchy of, 38
Aquitanian (language), 34
Aragon, 40
  Kingdom of Aragon, 30
Araitz Valley, 47, 50, 54
Aralar, 15, 26, 47, 54
Arberoue, 3
Arcal, Narbona d', 40
Archivo Real y General de Navarra (AGN), 3, 6–9, 48
Areso, Juan de, 48
Arles, Martin de, 14, 44
Armagnac, 41, 42

Armendarits, 3
Arriba, 54
Artieda, Martin de (Governor of Navarre), 6
At, Guilhem Rainol d', 34
Avignon, 7
Aymar, Esclarmonda, 21, 22
Azurmendi, Mikel, 56

B
Baïgorry, 3
Balda, Marichiqui, 48, 49, 57
Baraibar, 47
Baraibar y Arangoa, Johana de, 47
Barazarte, Martin de, 48, 56
Barbaste (family), 28
Barcelona, 20, 46
Barcelos, Pedro Afonso de, 46
Barheix, mistress of, 30
Basque (language), 3, 25–27, 34, 37, 48, 56
baton, 32, 33
Béarn, 27, 39
   Viscounty of Béarn, 6
Beheythie, Condesse de, vii, 6–14, 18–20, 22, 23, 25, 27, 58, 59, 65–70, 72
Benevento, 60
Bercebut, 54
Beunza, Maria Gracia de, 15
Biscay Hiriart, 19, 20, 67
Biterna, 34–36, 42
boc, bouc. See buck goat, he-goat
Boc de Biterna, 34, 36–41, 60
boque lane, boquelane, 25–27, 55, 58, 59, 68
Bordes, François, 27, 44
Brancion, Clara de, 28
Brancion, Ernesto de, 28
Breton (language), 35
Briggs, Robin, 1

Brittany, 35
broth, 14, 23, 42
buck goat, he-goat, 26, 30, 31, 33, 34, 38–40, 50, 55, 59, 60
buck sheep, 59
bufotenine, 25
Bunus, 30

C
Çamarguinarena, Gracia de, 54
Çamarguinarena, Juanes de, 54
Cambrue, Estebene de, 45, 46, 56
Camins, Sança de, 20
Camou, 19, 28, 29, 67
Camou, Tristan de (Bailiff of Mixe), 28, 29
Canon Episcopi, 14
Castelldefels, 46
Castell, Pau, 36, 38
Catalonia, 36, 59, 60
Cathars, 32, 43
Catholic Monarchs, 40
Caupenne, Archambault de, 45
Chabannes, Adémar de, 31
Chalosse, 44
Charnay, Annie, 17
Charter of Cuenca, 11
child-killing. *See* infanticide
Ciboure, 15
Cierbide, Ricardo, 28
Ciganda, Roberto, 9, 65
Cize, 3, 5
cock, 24
Cohn, Norman, 7, 8
crane, 30, 39, 42

D
Damascus, John of, 16
Dauphiny, 37
Devil, 14, 31, 38–40, 45, 46, 59
Deviless, 44, 46, 56

Diana, 14, 44
domina ludi. *See* Oriente, Madonna
Du Cange, 38
Du Pré, André, 41
Durango, 55

E
Echeandi, Maria de, 52
Echenique, Graxiana de, 52
Eliçague, Domenge d', 7, 10, 13, 14, 19, 22, 65, 67, 70
Eliçague, Guixon d', 7, 10, 13, 14, 65, 70
Engordany, 21
Errazkin, 54
Esparça, Johan Periz d', 72
Espina, Alonso de, 37, 38
Etchaluçuvi, Willem Arnaut d', 22, 23, 67, 68
Europe, 7
Eyherabide, Condeix d', 29, 30

F
Farreny, Maria Dolors, 39, 56
faytiler, faytilhera, 5, 7, 10, 17, 22, 29, 31, 40, 41, 65–70
faytiles, faytilhes, 10, 18, 22–24, 65–68, 70
fern, 22, 23, 25
  lady fern (*athyrium filix-femina*), 25
Folcaut, Bernat (Bishop of Pamplona), 7
France, 5, 35
  Kingdom of France, 38
Francesco, Matteuccia di, 59, 60
Franc, Martin le, 33
Froissart, Jean, 26
Fründ, Hans, 59
Fuero General de Navarra. *See* General Charter of Navarre

G
Gabat, 22, 23, 66–68
Garris, 5, 9, 18, 28, 29, 65, 66, 70
Garros, Jean de, 42, 43
Garros, Pey de, 42
Gascon-Occitan (language), 3, 6, 8, 9, 20, 26–28, 35, 43, 45, 46
Gascony, 26, 38, 41
General Charter of Navarre, 9, 10
Gipuzkoa, 15
goat, 24, 41, 47
Gourdon-en-Quercy, 5, 17, 19, 43
Goyheneche, Eugène, 6–8
Guarner, Valentina, 39, 41
Guida, Maria, 21
Guimarães, 31
Guoythie, Pes (or Pethri) de, vii, 6–14, 18–20, 22, 23, 30, 58, 65–70, 72

H
hallucinogen, 24, 25
harmaline, 25
harmine, 25
Hautes-Alpes, 33
Henningsen, Gustav, 56
herbolera, herbolaria, 5, 11
heresy, 31
Herodia, 14
Hingoue, Per Arnaut de, 19, 22, 23
hot iron ordeal, 7, 10, 11, 58
Huesca, 40
Hurcoyn, 10, 70, 72

I
Idoate, Florencio, 7, 8, 48, 55
Ihirçe, 19, 67
Iholdy, 3
Ilharrart, Peyrone d', 6, 12
Ilharrart, Willem Arnaut d', 6, 7, 9, 10, 12, 13, 18–20, 22, 23, 65–70

Ilharre, 6, 13, 14, 18–20, 22, 23, 45, 65, 72
infanticide, 7, 13, 14, 16, 18–23, 40, 54, 59, 60
initiation (into sorcery or witchcraft), 18, 29, 48, 57, 58
inquisitorial process, 29
Intza, 47, 50, 54, 56
Ireland, 24
Iriart, mistress of, 30
Iribarnaitzin, Marie d', 30
Irissarry, 3
Italy, 59
Ituren, 55

J
Juxue, 28–31

K
Kyteler, Alice, 24

L
La Bastide-Clairence, 5
  Bailiwick of La Bastide-Clairence, 3
Labourd, 15
Labrouche, Paul, 28
Lacxaga, Bernat Santz de (Bailiff of Mixe), 6, 8, 13, 72
Lafaurie, Léon de, 28
Lancre, Pierre de, 15, 45, 46, 56
Landemont, L'abbé (Pierre de Larremendy), 27–30, 56
Lands beyond the Ports. *See* Navarre, Lower Navarre
Lane de Boc, 26, 27, 30, 31, 39–42, 45, 46, 55, 56, 58
Lannemezan, 26
Lantabat, 3
Larboust Valley, 34

Larremendy, Pierre de. *See* Landemont, L'abbé (Pierre de Larremendy)
Lausanne, 32, 33
Lectoure, 41
Lizaso, 53
Lleida, 20, 39
Lodosa, Fermin de (Lord of Andueza and Perpetual Mayor of the Araitz Valley), 47, 48, 54
Lopez, Diego (Lord of Biscay), 46
Luciferum maiorem, 60

M
Magret, Guilhem, 34
maleficia (collectively performed), 23, 59
Manicheans, 31
Map, Walter, 31
Marca, Pierre de, 26
Marensin, 44
Mari, 47
Maugetaz, Aymonet, 33
Maya, 47
May de Biterna, 41–43
Meath, Petronilla of, 24
Mendaurre, 55
Mendiry, Jeanne de, 28
metamorphosis, 7, 8, 13–18, 23, 42, 44, 53, 59
  into a cat, 14, 15, 24, 42, 54
  into a dog, 7, 13–16, 24, 54
  into a fly, 60
  into a pig, 42
  into a wolf, 15, 59
  into an ass, 42
  into an owl, 16
Meung, Jean de, 17
milfoil. *See* yarrow (*achillea millefolium*)
Millau, 37

Mirepoix, 37
Mixe, 3, 5, 6, 8–11, 18, 27–29, 59
   Court of Mixe, 6, 8–11, 13, 28, 31
Mollera, Joan de, 46

N
Nagyvárad (Hungary), 11
Naquole, Menaut de (Lieutenant of the Bailiff of Mixe), 18, 66, 67
Navarre
   Court of Navarre, 8, 12, 66, 70
   Kingdom of Navarre, 2, 3, 10, 11, 44
   Lower Navarre, vii, 3, 4, 6, 27, 33, 39, 44
   Upper Navarre, 6, 15, 47, 50
Navarrese Romance (language), 3, 6
Negueloa, mistress of, 30
Nicholas V (pope), 38
Nider, Johannes, 44
Nigri, Hugo (inquisitor), 38

O
Oihenart, Arnaud, 28
ointment, 14–16, 20–24, 32, 36, 39–41, 49, 59, 60
Olagüe, Martin de, 52
Olagüe, Miguel de, 52
oleander (*nerium oleander*), 21, 22
Oradea (Romania), 11
ordeal. *See* hot iron ordeal
Orexa, Maria Miguel de, 47–51, 53–57
Oriente, Madonna, 57
Orkoien. *See* Hurcoyn
Orleans, 31
Orsoa, Jeanne d', 28
Ossès, 3
Ostabarret, 3, 28, 29
Ostitz, 15
Ovid, 16

P
Palay, Simin, 35, 42
Pamphile, 16
Pamplona, 3, 7, 8, 10, 12, 35, 47, 48, 53, 56, 72
Papias the Lombard, 38
Paul, Juainas, 55, 56
Perugorri, Juan Martiniz de, 53
Perugorri, Mari Hernandoiz de, 53
Picassany, Menaut de, 12, 13, 18, 68
pich sobre fulla, 39, 41, 46
Pierina, 57, 58
Piniès, Jean Pierre, 41
poison, 18, 20–25, 30, 38, 40, 60
Pont de Suert, 39
Portugal, 31
publicani, 31
Pyrenees, 3, 5, 6, 14, 15, 20, 33, 34, 37, 38, 44, 46

Q
Queen. *See* Valois, Joan of (Queen Regent)

R
Regestrum Varadinense, 11
Roig, Jaume, 36
Rome, 24
Royal and General Archive of Navarre. *See* Archivo Real y General de Navarra (AGN)

S
Sabbath, 15, 30, 45, 46
Sacaze, Julien, 34
Saint-Jean-Pied-de-Port, 5
   Castellany of Saint-Jean, 3
Saint-Malo, 35
Saint-Miqueu, mistress of, 30
Saint-Palais, 28

Sala, Johannette de, 28–31, 44
Salatipia, 29
San Sebastian, 7
Sarhie, Arnaud-Peloton de (Bailiff of Ostabarret), 29
Sarricoete, 20, 67
Satan. *See* Devil
scorpion, 24
Sibillia, 57
Siena, Bernardino de, 24
Solchaga, Martin Periz de, 72
Soler, Margarida, 21
sorgina, 37
Sorguinariçaga, 37
Sormendi, Johan de (procurator of the Lord of Mixe), 8, 9, 11, 67, 72
soul (leaving the body), 16, 17, 19, 41
Spanish Inquisition, 48
spider, 24
stake, 5, 23, 31, 37
strix, 16, 17
Sturluson, Snorri, 16
Switzerland, 59
synagogue, 31, 33, 35

T
Tartas, Viscount of, 3
toad, 22, 23, 25, 42, 59
Todi, 59
torture, 12, 13, 18, 29, 59, 70
Toulouse, 37

U
Ultzama, 15
Urriçola, 50
Urruthie, Bernat Santz d', 18, 27, 66–68

V
Valais, 59
Valencia, 36
Vallouise Valley. *See* Valpute
Valois, Joan of (Queen Regent), 6–9, 72
Valpute, 33
Vaschonia, Vasconia, 37, 38
Viana, 6
Viu, Jimeno de, 40

W
Waldensians, 32
Wilde, Oscar, 60
witch taster, 47
Wittgenstein, Ludwig, 58

Y
yarrow (*achillea millefolium*), 24

Z
Zaragoza, 40
Ziga, 52, 53
Zugarramurdi, 53

GPSR Compliance

The European Union's (EU) General Product Safety Regulation (GPSR) is a set of rules that requires consumer products to be safe and our obligations to ensure this.

If you have any concerns about our products, you can contact us on

ProductSafety@springernature.com

In case Publisher is established outside the EU, the EU authorized representative is:

Springer Nature Customer Service Center GmbH
Europaplatz 3
69115 Heidelberg, Germany